T0148814

PENGUIN BOOKS
WHY WE FEEL BLUE WHEN THE AIR IS GREY?

Sumit Agarwal is the Low Tuck Kwong Professor at the School of Business and professor in the departments of economics, finance, and real estate at the National University of Singapore (NUS). He is the managing director of Sustainable and Green Finance Institute at NUS. He is also the president of Asian Bureau of Finance and Economic Research. He has been a senior financial economist in the research department at the Federal Reserve Bank of Chicago and a senior vice president and credit risk management executive in the Small Business Risk Solutions Group of Bank of America. He has published over 125 research articles in economics and finance journals, including *American Economic Review, the Quarterly Journal of Economics,* and *Journal of Political Economics,* among others.

Agarwal is the associate editor of *Management Science, Journal of Financial Stability,* and *Journal of Financial Services Research.* Additionally, he has co-written four books titled *Introduction to Household Financial Management, Household Finance: A Functional Approach, Kiasunomics,* and *Kiasunomics 2.* He regularly writes op-eds in *The Straits Times* and features on various media outlets like the BBC, CNBC, and Fox to discuss issues related to finance, banking, and real estate markets. Agarwal's research has been widely cited in leading newspapers and magazines like the *Wall Street Journal, The New York Times, The Economist,* and the *US Presidents Report to Congress.*

Long Wang is an assistant professor at the School of Economics of Fudan University. His research interests lie in urban economics, environmental economics, and the Chinese economy. Wang received a PhD in real estate from the NUS in 2018, an MA in economics in 2013, and a BSc in mathematics in 2010 from Southwestern University of Finance and Economics. He has published in leading academic journals such as *The Review of Economics and Statistics, Journal of Public Economics,* and *Journal of Urban Economics,* among others.

Wang is the associate editor of *Regional Science and Urban Economics* and the principal investigator of the National Natural Science Foundation of China's Young Scientists Fund. He regularly writes opinion pieces and reports for the government, and his research findings have been featured various media outlets, including Economic Digest, Sing Tao Daily News, China Business Knowledge, and VoxChina, among others.

Yang Yang is an assistant professor at CUHK Business School of The Chinese University of Hong Kong. Her research focuses on urban economics, real estate, and sustainability. She has a PhD in real estate from the NUS (2018), an MSc in urban land economics (2014), and a BComm with honours in finance and real estate (2012) from the University of British Columbia. Her work has been published in leading academic journals such as *The Review of Economics and Statistics, Journal of Public Economics, Journal of Urban Economics,* among others.

Yang is the associate editor of *Regional Science and Urban Economics,* an academic editor for *PLOS One,* and sits on the editorial board of the *Journal of Real Estate Literature.* She is the principal investigator of several Hong Kong GRC projects and the National Natural Science Foundation of China's Young Scientists Fund. Yang writes op-ed pieces for *China Daily and Hong Kong Economic Journal* and she has been interviewed by various media organizations such as BBC Chinese, Fortune, Economic Daily, VICE and Quartz. Her research findings have been highlighted in a range of media outlets, including Economic Digest, China Business Knowledge, and VoxChina, among others.

Why We Feel Blue When the Air Is Grey?

Sumit Agarwal, Long Wang,
Yang Yang

PENGUIN BOOKS

An imprint of Penguin Random House

PENGUIN BOOKS

USA | Canada | UK | Ireland | Australia
New Zealand | India | South Africa | China | Southeast Asia

Penguin Books is part of the Penguin Random House group of companies
whose addresses can be found at global.penguinrandomhouse.com

Published by Penguin Random House SEA Pte Ltd
9, Changi South Street 3, Level 08-01,
Singapore 486361

Penguin
Random House
SEA

First published in Penguin Books by Penguin Random House SEA 2024
Copyright © Sumit Agarwal, Long Wang, Yang Yang 2024

ISBN 9789815017861

Typeset in Garamond by MAP Systems, Bengaluru, India

www.penguin.sg

Contents

Contents

Chapter 1

Breathing in the Haze: Understanding Air Pollution and Solutions

On a busy Monday morning, Ian headed to the university in Beijing to meet a renowned environmental expert who specialized in studying the city's air pollution and its effects on the environment. Ian was eager to discuss the ongoing challenges that the city faced as well as potential solutions to mitigate its effects. As he rode on the crowded subway, memories of his childhood spent exploring the natural world came flooding back to him, reminding him of his deep-rooted interest in environmental issues.

Growing up in a small countryside town, Ian was captivated by the wonders of the natural world from a young age. He would often lose himself in the woods, fields, and streams surrounding his home, exploring tirelessly, discovering new and fascinating plants and animals along the way. Through his explorations, Ian developed a deep appreciation for the complexity and beauty of the ecosystem. One of his fondest memories was spending time with his friends in the nearby river, where they would swim, splash around, and catch small fish in the crystal-clear water.

As Ian grew older, he started noticing disturbing changes in his beloved natural surroundings. The once-clear river that brought him so much joy and wonder had turned murky and polluted due to the factories that had popped up along its banks. The fish that he used to catch were now scarce and harder to come by. The air he breathed, once so fresh and invigorating, had become thick with pollutants from the nearby industries, making it difficult to take deep breaths. The pristine countryside that Ian once cherished was now contaminated with chemicals and toxins. Ian's memories of playing in the river and enjoying the natural beauty around him were cherished, but they became more distant as the water and air quality deteriorated over time. These experiences had a profound impact on Ian, and he became increasingly concerned about the impact of human activity on the environment.

Ian's passion for environmental issues deepened during his college years, where he studied journalism and began to explore ways to use his skills to make a positive impact on the world. He became an advocate for environmentally responsible living, urging his family and friends to reduce their carbon footprint and to make changes in their own lives. After graduation, he decided to pursue a career in journalism in Beijing, the capital city of China, hoping to use this platform to raise awareness about environmental issues.

Beijing, with a population of over twenty-one million people, is among the world's most populous cities and unfortunately, it is also notorious for its poor air quality. Despite the city's efforts to curb pollution, threats to the health of its residents persist due to factors such as vehicle emissions, coal-fired power plants, manufacturing, and population growth.

However, there have been notable advancements in Beijing's air quality in recent years. One significant achievement is the substantial 47 per cent decline in PM2.5 levels, a harmful air pollutant, between 2005 and 2015. PM2.5 refers to fine particulate matter with a diameter of less than 2.5 micrometres, which can penetrate deep into the lungs and even enter the bloodstream.

These tiny particles are generated by various sources, including combustion from cars, factories, and power plants, as well as dust and chemical reactions in the atmosphere.

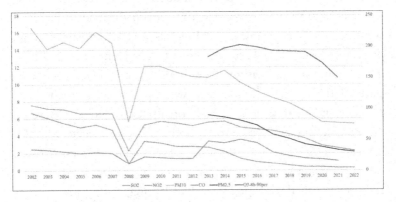

Figure 1.1: Changes in annual average concentrations
of major air pollutants in Beijing, 2002–22

Source: Figure based on data collected from the annual Report on the State of the Ecology and Environment in Beijing (2002–22) published by Beijing Municipal Ecology and Environment Bureau.

Note: This line chart displays the twenty-year changes in air pollutant concentrations in Beijing. It includes measurements of SO_2, NO_2, PM10, CO, PM2.5, and O3-8h-90per. The left vertical axis represents concentrations in mg/m3, while the right vertical axis represents concentrations in µg/m3. Starting from 2013, the chart includes data on PM2.5 concentration as monitoring began in 2012. However, please note that the chart does not include the annual average CO concentration for 2022 due to the unavailability of data from the source's unpublished report.

Despite the commendable reduction in PM2.5 levels, it is important to understand the nature of particulate matter. It is a combination of solid and liquid particles that come in different sizes. Particles can be divided into two types: fine particulate matter (smaller than 2.5 µg/m3) and coarse particulate matter (measuring between 2.5 and 10 µg/m3). Coarse PM can enter the lungs, while fine PM can enter the bloodstream once it passes through the lung barrier. The primary cause of PM pollution is the burning of fossil fuels in power plants, industries, and vehicles. These particles, due to their small size, can remain suspended in the air for extended periods and travel long distances. Exposure to high concentrations of PM2.5 can result in severe health outcomes. These can manifest within a few hours of prolonged exposure, particularly among individuals with pre-existing respiratory or cardiovascular diseases. Additionally, extended exposure to elevated levels of PM2.5 may trigger further negative health effects—ranging from asthma to heart attacks—or even cause death (Pope, et al., 2002; Auchincloss et al., 2008). In areas with high levels of PM2.5 pollution like Beijing, taking precautions such as wearing masks and limiting outdoor activities becomes crucial to protecting one's health.

The reduction in PM2.5 levels indicates a significant decrease in the concentration of these detrimental particles within the city's air. However, to achieve a substantial enhancement in Beijing's air quality and provide optimal breathing conditions for its inhabitants, further endeavours and progress are still necessary.

According to data from IQAir, Beijing's air quality was categorized as 'Unhealthy for Sensitive Groups' for ten months in 2019, with only two months classified as 'Moderate'. While this is an improvement from previous years, the city still has a long way to go to ensure healthy air quality for all its residents. But the Chinese government's efforts to tackle air pollution give us hope. Promoting the use of natural gas in power stations, encouraging the use of electric vehicles, and halting deforestation in the country have already led to some successes. In August 2019, Beijing recorded its lowest-ever monthly reading for air pollution, an encouraging sign that the situation is improving.

Despite these improvements, Beijing still ranks among the twenty cities in the world with the worst air quality, with sixteen of those cities located in China. As a result, the country's Environmental Sustainability Index ranks among the lowest globally. But with sustained efforts to tackle pollution and promote sustainable practices, Beijing can become a beacon of hope for other cities grappling with air quality issues.

Ian still remembered that when he'd first arrived in Beijing in 2006, he was greeted by a severe sandstorm that left a gritty feeling in his eyes and mouth. Despite the occasional haze, he noticed that some days had better air quality than others. However, he could still feel a slight heaviness in the air when he breathed it in, which he knew was a sign of the city's ongoing struggle with air pollution. On particularly bad days, the air was thick with smog, and he could feel the pollution in his lungs every time he stepped outside. As someone who cared deeply about the environment, Ian was struck by the scale of the challenges facing the city and its residents. He was determined to do his part to bring attention to the issue, which led him to report on air pollution in Beijing and raise awareness about this critical issue.

Ian arrived at the university and headed straight to Professor He's office. Upon reaching the door, he raised his hand and knocked, the sound echoing through the corridor. After a brief pause, Professor He's voice broke the silence. He called out in a strong and clear tone, inviting Ian to come inside. Taking a moment to collect himself, Ian took a deep breath and turned the doorknob. The door swung open, revealing Professor He seated behind the desk. His eyes were fixed on the computer screen, diligently studying the data about the sandstorm that had recently occurred in the spring of 2023.

'Thank you for agreeing to speak with me, Professor,' Ian said, taking a seat.

'It's my pleasure,' Professor He replied, turning his attention towards Ian. 'What can I do for you?'

Ian explained his intention of writing an article about the recent sandstorm in Beijing, and that he wanted to get an expert's opinion on what had caused it. Professor He nodded thoughtfully and began to explain that sandstorms in Beijing were caused by a combination of natural and human factors. 'One of the primary natural factors is the Gobi Desert, which is located in the north and northwest regions of China and Mongolia,' Professor He said. 'Strong winds can pick up vast amounts of sand and dust particles from the Gobi Desert and carry them over long distances, sometimes reaching Beijing.'

In addition to natural factors, human activities such as deforestation and overgrazing in the surrounding regions had contributed to soil erosion, making it easier for sand and dust to be picked up by the wind. 'Climate change has also been a factor, with the region experiencing drier and hotter conditions in recent years, which can exacerbate desertification and contribute to more frequent sandstorms,' Professor He added.

As Professor He elaborated, Ian diligently recorded the details, learning that the recent sandstorm in Beijing resulted from a powerful cyclone originating in Inner Mongolia and moving towards northwestern China, spanning from northern Xinjiang to central and western Gansu. 'The winds were blowing at between eight to ten times stronger than is normal at this time of year,' Professor He said. 'The Beijing Meteorological Observatory issued a blue gale warning and a blue sand and dust warning to remind citizens to protect themselves against sand and dust.'

'What do you mean by a blue gale warning and a blue sand and dust warning?' Ian asked, intrigued.

Professor He responded, 'The Beijing Meteorological Observatory issues two warnings to notify citizens about specific weather conditions. The first is a "blue gale" warning, indicating the possibility of strong and gusty winds. These winds can reach high speeds and pose risks, especially outdoors. The warning aims to raise awareness and prompt residents to take precautions, securing loose objects that could be affected by the strong winds.'

He continued, 'The second warning is a "blue sand and dust" warning. It is issued when there is a chance of sandstorms or a significant presence of airborne dust particles in the area. Sand and dust storms can occur due to factors like strong winds carrying particles from dry regions or construction sites. Inhaling these particles can reduce air quality and pose health risks. The warning reminds citizens to protect themselves by wearing masks, minimizing outdoor activities, and sealing indoor spaces to prevent dust from entering.

'By issuing these warnings, the Beijing Meteorological Observatory aims to keep the public informed about potentially hazardous weather conditions. They urge citizens to take appropriate measures to stay safe from the effects of strong winds and airborne dust particles,' Professor He added.

'I see,' Ian said, absorbing the information. 'And what was the situation like in Beijing during the sandstorm?' Professor He shared the data that the highest PM10 concentration had been 6496 μg/m³ in the Beijing suburbs and several other readings were reportedly off the scale, putting the air quality firmly in the 'Hazardous' category.

Ian nodded in acknowledgment of the severity of the situation. 'I'm concerned,' he said, 'what is your assessment of the air quality when there are no sandstorms? Could you also enlighten me about the underlying factors contributing to air pollution in Beijing?'

Professor He pointed out that rapid development had put severe pressure on Beijing's air quality. Over the past two decades, the city's economy had grown tenfold, the number of vehicles has increased by 3.5 times, energy consumption has risen by nearly

90 per cent, and the population has grown by almost 80 per cent. Given these factors, it was clear that Beijing faced significant challenges in addressing its air pollution problem.

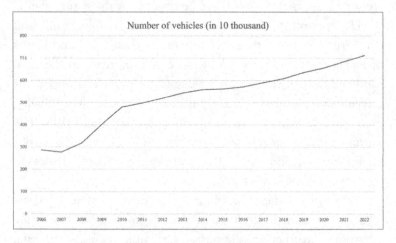

Figure 1.2: Number of vehicles in Beijing
from 2006–22 (in 10,000)

Source: The numbers of vehicles from 2006 to 2022 in Beijing are sourced from the Statistical Communiqué of Beijing, https://www.beijing.gov.cn (accessed October 20, 2023).

He continued, 'The pressure mainly comes from four areas. First, coal-related pollutant emissions, whether it is used for power generation, industry, or civilian purposes. In the past twenty years, especially in the early stages, coal consumption was very high. In 1998, the entire city consumed 28 million tons of coal per year. Second, motor vehicles, especially the increase in logistics and freight trucks. Third, industry, including steelmaking by Capital Iron and Steel Company before 2008 and now coke and chemical industrial parks in the eastern suburbs of Beijing. Fourth, construction and various road dust.'

'How has Beijing tackled these pollution pressures?' Ian asked Professor He.

'To combat pollution, especially the air pollution caused by coal and motor vehicles, Beijing has implemented a range of air improvement plans based on scientific research from universities and research institutes since 1998,' Professor He explained. 'These measures have been enshrined in local legislation and are closely monitored in real-time by over a 1000 air monitoring stations throughout the city.'

Professor He went on to add, 'Over the years, Beijing has made significant progress in reducing coal consumption. From burning 28 million tons of coal in 1998, the city's coal consumption has now dropped to about 4 million tons and is continuing to decrease towards a level of 2–3 million tons. To further reduce emissions, China has adopted "ultra-low emissions" standards in coal-fired power generation, which have helped to significantly reduce the release of harmful pollutants like particulate matter 10 (PM10), nitrogen oxides (NOx), and sulphur dioxide (SO_2), putting the country at the forefront of clean energy production. In terms of motor vehicles, Beijing was the first city in China to implement motor vehicle tailpipe emission standards, setting a new benchmark for other cities in the country to follow suit,' Professor He concluded.

SO_2 is a gas that is produced by burning fossil fuels containing sulphur, such as coal and oil. It can have negative impacts on both human health and the environment. Exposure to high levels of sulphur dioxide can irritate the eyes, nose, and throat, and can exacerbate asthma symptoms. It can also contribute to acid rain, which can harm forests, crops, and bodies of water. In order to reduce sulphur dioxide emissions, many countries have implemented regulations requiring the use of low-sulphur fuels and the installation of sulphur dioxide scrubbers in industrial facilities.

NO is a gas that is produced when fossil fuels are burned at high temperatures, such as in motor vehicle engines and power plants. Like sulphur dioxide, it can have negative impacts on human health and the environment. Exposure to nitrogen oxide can lead to respiratory problems, particularly in people with asthma or other lung conditions. Nitrogen oxide also contributes to the formation of ground-level ozone, which can harm plants and animals and reduce crop yields. To reduce nitrogen oxide emissions, many countries have implemented regulations requiring the use of catalytic converters in motor vehicles and the installation of nitrogen oxide scrubbers in industrial facilities.

PM10 refers to particulate matter that is 10 micrometres or less in diameter. These tiny particles can come from a variety of sources, including motor vehicle exhaust, industrial emissions, and dust from construction sites and unpaved roads. Exposure to PM10 can cause respiratory and cardiovascular problems, particularly in people with preexisting health conditions such as asthma or heart disease. To reduce PM10 emissions, many countries have implemented regulations requiring the use of particle filters in motor vehicles and the implementation of dust control measures at construction sites and other sources of particulate matter.

Ian listened to Professor He's words with great interest. He knew that the air quality in Beijing had been a serious problem for years, and he was glad to hear that there was progress being made.

'So, the concentration of sulphur dioxide, nitrogen oxide, and PM10 have significantly decreased?' Ian asked for clarification.

'Yes,' Professor He replied. 'Especially sulphur dioxide, which has decreased by 93 per cent from 1998 to 2017. In 1998, the winter levels of sulphur dioxide in Beijing would reach over 120, but the annual average sulphur dioxide was only 6 in 2022, dropping from over 100 to single digits. It shows that coal control has shown a very strong effect. Nitrogen dioxide has decreased by 38 per cent since 1998, and PM10 has also decreased by 55 per cent.'

Ian was impressed by the numbers. 'And what about PM2.5? It's what most concerns the Chinese people, right?'

'Exactly,' Professor He nodded. 'Since being included in the national standard for monitoring in 2013, PM2.5 has shown a gradual improvement. In 2013, there were four consecutive haze warnings in a week, dozens of highways were forced to close, and the record for the number of haze days was broken. But now, those days are behind us.

'PM2.5 has decreased by 35 per cent from 2013 to 2017 and 42 per cent from 2013 to 2018,' he continued. 'In 2013, Beijing's annual average PM2.5 value was 89, and last year it had dropped to 51, especially during the winter when the reduction was most apparent. The term "explosive" was used before to describe PM2.5 concentrations, but since about two years ago, Beijing has already controlled it and hasn't seen the situation of "explosive" for PM2.5. The whole of North China region has gradually been controlled as well.'

As for the duration of continuous pollution, it was also decreasing. Professor He said that while there would still be polluted days in winter, there had not been a continuous haze for three days in Beijing since last year. Days with PM2.5 concentrations at a medium to high level would still occur, but their duration had shortened. Therefore, the 'symptoms' of pollution were significantly alleviating, and this phenomenon was clear.

'But is the air quality in Beijing good now?' Ian asked.

Professor He answered, 'This question needs to be looked at from different perspectives.' He then provided some data to give a better understanding of the current air quality situation in Beijing. According to Professor He, the annual average concentration of

PM2.5 in Beijing in 2020 was 39, which was still above the national standard of China—as set by the World Health Organization (WHO)—of 35.

'While it's true that the annual average concentrations of PM2.5 and SO_2 in Beijing during the COVID-19 period were lower than before, this was likely due to reduced manufacturing activities and traffic resulting from mobility restrictions. When compared to major cities in the European Union, the average PM2.5 level is less than 15, and in major cities in the United States, the average level is in the single digits, below 10. Therefore, there is still a long way to go and much work to be done to improve the air quality in Beijing.' He continued.

Ian nodded thoughtfully and said, 'It's good news to hear that pollution levels are reducing, but there's still much to be done to keep up the progress towards better air quality, right?'

'Absolutely,' Professor He nodded in agreement. 'Although it's encouraging to see progress being made, we can't rest on our laurels just yet. There are still challenges to be tackled if we want to continue improving the air quality in Beijing. For instance, while we have seen a decline in some pollutants like PM2.5 and SO_2, others like ozone have actually increased in recent years.'

Ozone (O_3) is a gas that can be both beneficial and harmful. In the upper atmosphere, ozone protects us from harmful ultraviolet radiation from the sun. However, at ground level, ozone is a major component of air pollution and can harm human health, crops, and ecosystems. Ground-level ozone is formed when nitrogen oxides (NOx) and volatile organic compounds (VOCs) react in the presence of sunlight. These pollutants come from sources such as motor vehicle exhausts, industrial emissions, and gasoline vapours. When people are exposed to high levels of ozone, it can irritate the lungs, causing chest pain, coughing, and shortness of breath. Long-term exposure to ozone can also cause respiratory diseases, such as asthma, and increase the risk of premature death.

Ian frowned. 'That's definitely concerning. But what can be done to address these issues?'

'It's like playing whack-a-mole, you fix one problem, and another one pops up. It's a continuous battle that we have to fight. Furthermore, transportation and industry are still major sources of pollution that need to be addressed. It's not just about reducing emissions but also about finding alternative sources of energy that are sustainable in the long run. We need to work together as a society to make a positive impact on the environment, and that includes both individuals and businesses.'

Professor He leaned forward. 'There are a lot of solutions that can help us continue to improve air quality. For example, we can promote the use of cleaner energy sources, like natural gas or renewable energy. We can also work on improving public transportation to reduce the number of cars on the road. And we can implement stricter regulations on industry to ensure they're not releasing harmful pollutants into the air.'

Ian's face brightened as he listened to Professor He's suggestions for improving air quality. 'It's great to hear that there are so many solutions available,' he said. 'But how can we ensure that these solutions are implemented effectively?'

Professor He nodded thoughtfully. 'One of the most important things we can do is to educate people about the impact of air pollution on different aspects of daily life, such as our health, the economy, and the environment. But it's not just limited to these areas. Air pollution can also have a significant impact on other aspects of human behaviour, such as decision-making, emotion, and consumption habits. Studies have shown that exposure to air pollution can impair cognitive function, leading to poor decision-making and decreased productivity. It can also lead to increased stress and anxiety, as well as negative emotions such as anger and sadness. Also, air pollution can impact our consumption habits, as people may choose to avoid certain activities or products due to concerns about air quality.'

Ian looked surprised. 'Wow, that's quite eye-opening. I had no idea that air pollution could have such a far-reaching impact on our lives beyond just the obvious health and environmental concerns. It really emphasizes the importance of taking action to reduce pollution levels. I think education is key, not just for raising awareness about the issue, but also for empowering individuals to make informed decisions and take steps to reduce their own carbon footprint. I'm definitely going to be more conscious of the air quality around me and try to make choices that contribute to a cleaner and healthier environment.'

'Exactly,' Professor He nodded in agreement. 'By educating people about the impact of air pollution on different aspects of their lives, we can encourage them to make changes in their daily habits that can help reduce pollution levels. For example, people may choose to walk or bike instead of driving or opt for public transportation instead of using their own vehicles. They may also choose to purchase products and services from companies that prioritize sustainability and eco-friendliness. These small changes can add up and make a big difference in improving the air quality of our cities. But most importantly, it's about making a commitment to sustainability and being willing to make changes, even if they may be inconvenient at first.'

Ian listened intently, 'That makes sense. What else can be done?'

Professor He continued, 'Governments can also implement stricter regulations on industry to ensure they're not releasing harmful pollutants into the air. For example, they can require companies to use cleaner production methods and technologies and enforce penalties for violations. Additionally, governments can promote the use of public transportation and encourage people to use bikes or walk more often to reduce the number of cars on the road.'

Ian nodded, 'That all sounds like it would make a big difference. But what can companies do to reduce air pollution?'

Professor He replied, 'Companies can take steps to reduce their environmental impact by adopting sustainable practices. This can include reducing waste, conserving energy, and using eco-friendly materials. They can also invest in clean technology, such as electric vehicles or renewable energy sources. Companies can work to reduce their carbon footprint by using more efficient transportation methods, like shipping products by rail instead of truck.'

Ian grinned, feeling a renewed sense of optimism. 'It's great to hear that there are concrete actions that everyone can take to make a positive impact on air quality. It's easy to feel overwhelmed by the scale of the problem but knowing that there are practical solutions out there makes me feel hopeful for the future.'

'Absolutely,' Professor He replied, a smile illuminating his face. 'It's essential for each of us to play a part in improving the air quality in our cities. By taking action, we not only improve our own lives but also leave a lasting impact for future generations.'

Feeling a surge of inspiration, Ian rose from his seat. 'Thank you, Professor He. This conversation has truly ignited a fire within me to make a difference and contribute to enhancing air quality in our cities.'

Professor He's eyes sparkled with enthusiasm. 'You're most welcome, Ian. It's always refreshing to connect with individuals who genuinely care about the environment and the future of our city.'

As their discussion drew to a close, Ian felt a newfound curiosity and determination taking hold. The chapter on air quality was just the beginning of his quest for knowledge. He yearned to delve deeper into understanding the impact of air pollution and its far-reaching consequences.

Chapter 2

Choking on the Air: How Pollution Affects Body and Mind

It was a bright Monday morning, and Jenny was feeling anxious as she paced around her living room. She had been researching primary schools for weeks now, and she had finally narrowed it down to two options. The first option was a bilingual school that had won multiple awards, but its location near the highway raised concerns about air pollution. The second option was more standard, but it boasted a beautiful botanical garden nearby and better air quality. Jenny was torn between the two and couldn't decide which one to choose. She knew that her son's education was crucial, but she also wanted him to be in a safe and healthy environment.

Jenny felt a bit nervous as she contemplated making the final decision, which was a significant milestone for her son. She wanted to ensure that she made the right choice, so she decided to call up her friend Ian for some guidance. Ian was always dependable and had a way of putting things into perspective, which was precisely what Jenny needed right now.

'Hey, Jenny. What's up?' Ian asked as he picked up the phone.

'Hey, Ian. I need your help,' Jenny replied, her voice quivering with anxiety. 'I'm trying to decide which school to send my son to, but I just can't seem to make up my mind. One has a better reputation, but it's near the highway, and the other is just an ordinary school, but it's close to the Beijing Botanical Garden with better air quality.' Ian listened attentively and understood her dilemma.

'Jenny, I understand how tough this decision must be for you,' Ian replied, empathizing with her anxiety. 'I think it would be a good idea for us to visit both schools and see them for ourselves. That way, you can have all the information you need before making your decision.'

Ian's suggestion brought a visible sense of relief to Jenny, who let out a sigh. She considered Ian's proposal and then asked, 'Do you know anyone who could help us understand the air quality near the schools?'

Ian pondered for a moment, thinking of potential contacts who could provide valuable insights. Finally, he responded, 'Actually, I have a friend named Ethan who works at the research centre of the medical school. He specializes in air quality research. Let me give him a call and see if he can join us on the tour. His scientific expertise would be incredibly helpful in understanding the air quality around both schools.'

Jenny's face lit up. 'That would be amazing, Ian! Thank you so much,' she said gratefully.

Ian quickly called Ethan and explained the situation.

'I'd be happy to help out,' Ethan said. 'I can meet you both at the schools and give you some information on air pollution and its effects on children.'

The next day, Ian, Ethan, and Jenny drove to visit the first school on their list. During the drive, Ian noticed the traffic pollution and remarked, 'It's strange,' he said, 'how despite all the advancements in technology, we still can't seem to get a handle on traffic pollution.'

Ethan, who had been studying the issue, jumped in. 'Actually, I've been reading about this,' he said. 'There's a recent study by Alexander and Schwandt that talks about the impact of car pollution on infant and child health.'

Jenny, who was interested in the topic, asked Ethan to elaborate.

Ethan explained, 'With car exhaust being a major source of air pollution, several problems on population health are induced with the increase of PM2.5, PM10, and ozone emissions, including low birth weight rate and infant mortality rate, which subsequently impact gestation rate and even birth outcomes,' he said.

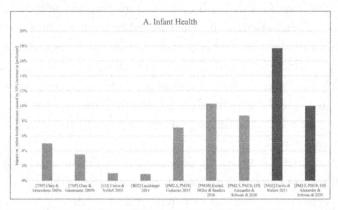

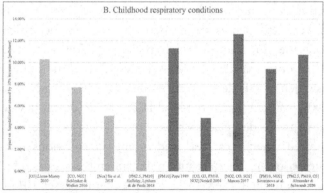

Figure 2.1: Quasi-experimental estimates of the per cent change in infant health and childhood respiratory conditions associated with a 10 per cent change in pollution

Source: Alexander, D., and Schwandt, H. (2022). 'The Impact of Car Pollution on Infant and Child Health: Evidence from Emissions Cheating.' *The Review of Economic Studies*, 89(6), 2872–910.

'In the study, scholars also pointed out how diesel cars that are seemingly more environmentally friendly outweigh gasoline cars in terms of pollution, thus describing these diesel cars' "emission-cheating" in the paper's title and throughout the dissertation,' he added.

Jenny asked, 'What are the differences between diesel and gasoline vehicles?'

Ethan explained, 'Both diesel and gasoline are refined from crude oil, but diesel is heavier and oilier than gasoline, with a longer carbon chain and higher energy density. This means that diesel engines are more efficient and emit less carbon dioxide, which is a greenhouse gas. However, diesel fuel emits more nitrogen oxides and particulate matter, which can cause smog and negatively affect lung function, leading to respiratory diseases and even mortality.'

The mid-2000s saw the development of a new diesel engine, TDI Clean Diesel, by Volkswagen engineers to meet the stringent US emissions standards for passenger vehicles. Volkswagen advertised this new diesel line as having all the benefits of diesel vehicles, such as strong performance and fuel efficiency, without the downside of high pollution. However, in 2015, the Environmental Protection Agency (EPA) made public that Volkswagen's TDI Clean Diesel models were emitting NOx at up to 4,000 per cent above the legal limit due to 'defeat devices'— illegal software designed to cheat emissions tests. The software recognized when a car was undergoing an emissions test and adjusted components to reduce pollutant emissions to compliant levels. As a result, these vehicles had previously passed EPA drive cycle tests. The EPA's investigation into Volkswagen's TDI Clean Diesel cars led to the conclusion that Fiat Chrysler Automobiles (FCA)'s EcoDiesel engine contained similar illegal software. This diesel emission cheating scandal resulted in Volkswagen and

FCA being fined billions of dollars and facing legal action from affected customers.

Ian's curiosity was sparked by the study, and he asked eagerly, 'What kind of data did they use? Did they conduct any experimental research, or did they solely rely on previous studies? And could you provide more insights into their investigation process?'

Ethan explained that the research gathered year by year data including vehicle registration, pollution, birth data, and emergency department discharge. 'Other data such as median income, poverty, and vehicle-miles driven are also collected for investigation in terms of universal vehicle registrations,' he said.

'The major findings were that a cheating diesel car per 1000 cars results in a 2 per cent and 2.2 per cent increase in PM2.5 and PM10 emissions, a 1.3 per cent increase in ground-level ozone, a 1.9 per cent increase in the rate of low birth weight, and a 1.7 per cent increase in infant mortality rate,' he added.

Jenny was concerned about the impact on infants and children. 'What does that mean for their health?' she asked.

Ethan explained that the study found that the 612,892 TDI cars sold from 2008 to 2015 were estimated to result in approximately 38,686 infants with low birth weights and approximately 290 deaths in infants. 'This is a serious issue that needs to be addressed,' he said.

Ian was shocked and asked, 'What are the implications of the study?'

Ethan responded, stressing the importance of regulating vehicle pollution and developing cleaner technologies to mitigate the significant impact of air pollution on infant and child health. He emphasized that raising public awareness about the potential health risks associated with diesel cars is crucial. Ian concurred, stating that the impact was alarming, and measures needed to be taken to reduce traffic pollution and its harmful effects on public health.

Jenny chimed in with a suggestion to explore alternative modes of transportation, such as cycling or walking, as a starting point to reducing traffic pollution. While this might not be practical for everyone, it could be a small step in the right direction.

'It's amazing how rapidly China's economy has grown over the past few decades. They've become a major player in the global market and have even set a goal of becoming the world leader by 2050,' Ian said.

Jenny nodded in agreement, 'Yes, it's impressive, but I can't help but wonder about the impact of their economic growth on the environment.'

Ethan chimed in, 'Exactly. China's pollution problem is well known, and it could be a major obstacle to their ambition of being a world leader.'

Ian nodded, 'I agree. We need to address our environmental issues if we want to maintain our economic growth.'

'Hey, have you guys heard about the research conducted by Professor Ebenstein and his collaborators back in 2015? It's a fascinating study that explores the relationship between China's economic growth, pollution levels, and life expectancy. They delved into years of data, from 1991 to 2012, shedding light on this intriguing topic,' Ethan said. This research provides a comprehensive analysis of the consequences of China's rapid economic expansion and highlights the potential trade-offs that may arise between economic growth and environmental sustainability.

Table 2.1: Trends in health, income, and
pollution in China, 1991–2012

	1991	2000	2012
Life expectancy at birth	69.3 (6.6)	71.5 (5.6)	75.7 (3.5)
Life expectancy at age 5	67.1 (5.9)	68.1 (5.1)	71.4 (3.3)
All-cause mortality (per 100,000)	863.4 (305.4)	821.2 (341.2)	531.7 (135.7)
Cardiorespiratory diseases	432 (214.8)	463.4 (236.6)	310.3 (100.1)
Non-cardiorespiratory diseases	431.5 (203.3)	357.8 (158.5)	221.4 (59.7)
GDP per capita (2010 yuan)	4,317 (2,167)	9,546 (5,320)	40,151 (16,052)
Particulate matter (PM10, μg/m3)	111.3 (41.8)	87.9 (44.4)	80.1 (21.0)

Source: Ebenstein, A., Fan, M., Greenstone, M., He, G., Yin, P., and Zhou, M. (2015). 'Growth, pollution, and life expectancy: China from 1991–2012.' *American Economic Review*, 105(5), 226–31.

'That sounds interesting,' Jenny said. 'What did they find?'

'The research found that there's a positive association between GDP and life expectancy, but a negative association between particulate matter pollution and life expectancy,' Ethan explained. 'Basically, pollution is causing an increase in mortality rates despite China's impressive economic growth.'

Ian expressed his curiosity and asked Ethan to elaborate on the research paper. Ethan went on to explain that the study drew upon the extensive data available from China's Disease Surveillance Points System (DSPS) EPA to examine mortality trends across different factors such as GDP per capita, income, health, and pollution. The findings of the study revealed that pollution had a direct impact on life expectancy, and indirectly affected income growth. The study found that while there was a general increase in life expectancy from 69.3 to 75.7 years between 1991 and 2012, the improvement was mainly observed in mortality rates of children under the age of five.

Ethan added. 'So, if pollution levels don't decrease, China's rapid development could be hindered.'

Ian chimed in. 'But we all noticed that there has been a significant decline in air pollutants in the past two decades, which is a positive sign.'

'Indeed,' Ethan nodded. 'Although particulate matter and sulphur dioxide levels have decreased significantly, surpassing other countries' reduction in pollution levels, the pollution problem is far from solved. The air quality in many Chinese cities still surpasses the WHO minimum safe level. We need to continue to address this issue to ensure continued economic growth and to improve health and life expectancy in the long run.'

Jenny nodded in agreement. 'I hope the Chinese government takes this issue seriously and implements policies to reduce pollution levels.'

In recent years, the severity of air pollution in Beijing has been extensively studied and documented. According to the Beijing Municipal Environmental Monitoring Center (2021), the average concentration of PM2.5 in Beijing in 2020 was 42 micrograms per cubic metre, which is more than four times the recommended limit of 10 micrograms per cubic metre set by WHO. This high level of pollution has resulted in a significant increase in respiratory and cardiovascular diseases, particularly among children.

Exposure to traffic-related air pollution poses a significant threat to the health of children and adults in both the short and long term. Research has consistently shown that exposure to pollutants like $PMNO_2$, SO_2 has been linked to respiratory and cardiovascular diseases, cognitive impairment, and even death. According to WHO (2018), air pollution is responsible for the deaths of approximately 600,000 children under five years of age every year worldwide.

Studies have consistently demonstrated the adverse health effects of exposure to traffic-related air pollution. Brunekreef and Holgate (2002) reported that exposure to air pollution is associated with a higher prevalence of asthma, chronic bronchitis, and pneumonia in children. Gauderman et al. (2015) found that children exposed to high levels of air pollution are more likely to develop lung function impairment and experience persistent wheezing. Moreover, Lelieveld et al. (2015) estimated that outdoor air pollution is responsible for approximately three million premature deaths globally each year. These findings highlight the urgent need for effective policies to reduce air pollution and protect public health.

'You know, I came across this paper called "What Do We Know About Short- and Long-Term Effects of Early-Life Exposure to Pollution?" and it reinforces what we've been discussing about the detrimental health effects of early-life pollution exposure,' Ethan shared, adding to their ongoing conversation. 'It's a systematic review that dives into the existing studies, examining both the short- and long-term impacts of early-life exposure to pollution.'

'That sounds interesting,' said Ian. 'What did they find?'

'Well, they found that exposure to air pollution during critical windows of development, such as pregnancy and early childhood, can lead to a variety of health problems later in life,' Ethan explained.

'That's really concerning,' said Jenny. 'But how severe are the effects?'

'They can be quite severe, especially for vulnerable populations such as low-income communities and ethnic minority groups,' Ethan replied. 'The study also found that exposure to pollution during these critical windows of development can have both short and long–term effects, which means that the effects can last a lifetime.'

Ian nodded thoughtfully. 'What kind of pollution are we talking about here?'

'Mainly air pollution,' Ethan said. 'But the study also looked at exposure to lead and other toxic chemicals, which can have similarly negative effects on health.'

Jenny looked concerned. 'So, what can we do to protect ourselves and our communities from these harmful effects?'

'Well, the study highlights the urgent need for policies and interventions that reduce pollution and protect the health of vulnerable populations,' Ethan replied.

The impact of air pollution on cognitive function and mental health is also a growing concern. Several studies have found a significant association between exposure to air pollution and cognitive impairment in children and adults. A prospective cohort study of primary school children in Barcelona found that exposure to traffic-related air pollution was associated with slower cognitive development (Sunyer et al., 2015). Another study found that exposure to high levels of air pollution can lead to decreased cognitive performance in adults (Zhang et al., 2018). The impact of air pollution on cognitive function can also have long-term effects on human capital formation, as suggested by a study conducted in Israel (Lavy et al., 2014). Moreover, recent research conducted in China found that air pollution is associated with an increased risk of depression and anxiety (Cao et al., 2023). These findings suggest that the negative impact of air pollution extends beyond physical health and can have significant effects on cognitive function and mental health.

Ethan shared valuable insights from Zhang et al., (2018). The study focused on exploring the connection between air pollution and cognitive performance in China. Ethan explained, 'Professor Zhang and his team found that exposure to air pollution has an impact on verbal tests, and interestingly, this effect becomes more pronounced as people age, especially for less educated men.'

Ian was concerned and asked, 'What kind of cognitive impairment are we talking about here?'

Ethan replied, 'The study focused on the relationship between air pollution and Alzheimer's disease and other forms of dementia for elderly persons. Cognitive decline is a risk factor for these diseases, and they can be quite costly. Alzheimer's disease alone cost $226 billion in health services and eighteen billion labour hours of unpaid caregiving in 2015.'

Ian looked at Ethan and asked, 'Have you come across any studies on pollution and children's health in other countries?'

'Actually, I remember a fascinating study that perfectly illustrates the impact of air pollution,' Ethan replied with a nod. 'There's a well-known study conducted by Chay and Greenstone in which they investigated the impact of air pollution on infant mortality. It provides valuable insights into this important topic.'

Ethan continued. 'It talks about how governments have regulated pollution levels to protect the public's health, especially when it comes to total suspended particulates, which are believed to be the most pernicious form of air pollution.'

Total suspended particulates (TSP) refer to the small solid or liquid particles suspended in the air that can have adverse effects on human health and the environment. These particles can come from a variety of sources, including transportation, power generation, and industrial processes. TSP can vary in size and composition, ranging from coarse particles such as dust and pollen to fine particles like soot and smoke. Exposure to high levels of TSP can cause respiratory problems, cardiovascular disease, and even premature death. Specifically, TSP is a measurement used to describe the total mass of particulate matter suspended in the air, including both PM2.5 and PM10. However, PM2.5 and PM10 specifically refer to the size range of particles. WHO recommends that the annual average concentration of TSP in the air should not exceed 90 micrograms per cubic metre. Many countries have regulations in place to monitor and control TSP levels to protect public health and the environment.

'Can you tell us more about the study?' asked Jenny.

Ethan took a deep breath before launching into a detailed explanation. 'Well, the paper examines the impact of pollution on infant mortality rates, specifically focusing on the relationships between air pollution from particulate matters and infant mortality in the United States between 1980 to 1982. During this period, PM pollution experienced substantial variations across different counties, inducing varying degrees of influence on infant mortality rates.'

Ian furrowed his brow. 'But what's so special about this period of time? Why did they focus on it?'

Ethan nodded, understanding his confusion. 'The time frame is driven by the recession in 1981 to 1982, which induced significant changes in pollution with geographical variations in a narrow time period. The recession contributed to drastic reductions in pollution levels of suspended particulates among sites, which were heavily industrialized with large numbers of manufacturing plants shut down during the period. Such an incident acted as a crucial cause for the improvements in air quality in areas nearby, while other locations without pollution-intensive manufacturing and industrialized sites nearby experienced mild and minimal changes in pollution data.'

Jenny's eyes lit up with interest as she leaned in towards Ethan. 'What exactly did they discover about the link between pollution and infant mortality?' she asked eagerly.

Ethan continued, 'They found that a reduction of 1 microgram per cubic metre among particulate matters would lead to approximately four to seven fewer deaths per 100,000 infants and live births. The data was gathered by examining county-level air pollution, economic conditions, characteristics, infant births, and infant deaths in 1978 to 1984, which helped identify the factors associated with infant mortality.'

As they approached the school, Jenny's attention was focused on its modern facilities and the bilingual programme on offer. However, stepping out of the car, they were immediately struck by the noise emanating from the nearby highway and the overpowering scent of exhaust fumes in the air. They walked around the school, observing the facilities, the teachers, and the children. The classrooms were bright and spacious, and the teachers seemed enthusiastic and caring. They also spoke with some of the parents and teachers to gather more information about the school and its programmes.

Ethan had brought along a device that measured air quality, and he recorded the readings as they walked around. 'The air pollution levels here are higher than what we would want to see, but still below the threshold that is considered unsafe,' Ethan explained. 'However, it's important to note that prolonged exposure to even slightly elevated pollution levels can have negative effects on the children's health.' Ethan's device confirmed that the air quality was not as good as it could be, highlighting the need for continued efforts to improve air quality in the area.

Jenny's heart sank as she listened to Ethan's report. Although her son had only experienced respiratory issues when he was very young, she remained concerned about his health, especially given the dangers of air pollution and its impact on young children. This worry had become a constant presence in her mind.

My son's health is my top priority. I cannot risk exposing him to harmful pollutants,' Jenny said.

Ethan empathized with Jenny's apprehension and quickly offered a solution. 'Don't worry. We can explore the neighbouring school's air quality and compare it to this one. That way, we can choose the best option for your son.'

They then headed to the second school, located near the botanic garden. The walk was peaceful, and the fresh air helped to ease Jenny's worries. The school was smaller than the first one, but it had a warm and welcoming atmosphere. The children were playing in a garden filled with colourful flowers and trees, and the sound of their laughter filled the air.

As they walked around, Ethan used his air quality monitor to check the levels of pollutants in the air. 'The air quality here is much better than the previous school,' he said.

As they walked through the garden, Ethan pointed out some of the different types of plants and flowers they were passing by. 'Did you know that some plants are actually better at filtering pollutants than others?' he asked, gesturing towards a row of bushes along the path. 'These boxwood shrubs are great at trapping particles and absorbing harmful gases like NO_2.'

Jenny was fascinated by this information and made a mental note to learn more about the plants in her own garden. 'That's amazing,' she said. 'I had no idea that plants could do so much to improve air quality.'

Ian nodded in agreement. 'It's really incredible how nature has its own way of cleaning up the air around us,' he said. 'We just need to do our part to protect it and help it thrive.'

As they continued walking, they came across a small pond filled with water lilies and koi fish. The children from the nearby school were gathered around, tossing breadcrumbs to the fish and giggling as they darted back and forth.

'This is such a peaceful place,' Jenny said, watching the children play. 'I can see why the air quality is so much better here. It's like we're in a little oasis in the middle of the city.'

Ethan watched the children playing in the lush green garden and smiled. He understood the importance of green spaces in promoting children's physical and mental health and knew that this was a place where children could not only have fun but also learn and grow.

'Clean air is crucial for children's physical and mental health,' Ethan emphasized, his gaze shifting towards the children playing in the garden. 'Green spaces like this help to filter the air, reducing exposure to harmful pollutants that can harm their developing respiratory and immune systems. Not only that, but these spaces also provide a safe and stimulating environment for children to explore and learn about the natural world around them, which can have a positive impact on their mental well-being.'

Jenny had been struggling to find the right school for her son that would provide a safe and healthy environment, but with Ethan's guidance and expertise, she felt relieved. She imagined her son playing in the garden, surrounded by fresh air and the beauty of nature. After visiting both schools and weighing the pros and cons, Jenny knew that choosing the school near the botanic garden was the right decision for her son's health and well-being. Although the other bilingual school had a strong academic reputation and was closer to home, Jenny realized that clean air was essential for her son's physical and mental health and didn't want to compromise on that. After talking with the school staff and seeing the facilities, she was convinced that this was the perfect place for her son. She enrolled him in the school, feeling happy and confident that he would receive a high-quality education in a safe and healthy environment, thanks to Ethan and Ian's help.

'Thank you so much for coming with me, guys,' Jenny said, feeling grateful for her friends' help. 'I really needed your help to make the right decision for my son.'

Ian grinned. 'Of course, we're always here for you,' he said.

Jenny nodded in agreement. She knew that her son would be in good hands at the school near the botanic garden and looked forward to watching him thrive and grow in his new environment. As they walked away from the school, she felt a sense of hope and optimism for her son's future.

Chapter 3

When Smoke Clouds the Lion City: The Impact of Wildfires

After the five-and-a-half-hour flight from Beijing Capital International Airport to Changi International Airport, Ian couldn't wait to view the stunning architecture and other beautiful attractions of Singapore. But the hazy sky he saw through the window of the airplane during the landing cooled his ardour.

'Bad luck! The haze is back!' exclaimed the lady beside Ian.

'Haze? In Singapore?' Ian was shocked.

Living in Beijing, he was no stranger to haze. For many years, the wintertime air in Beijing has been choked by a dusty and toxic haze. Due to intensive industrialization, the Beijing–Tianjin–Hebei region is one of the most heavily polluted areas of China. Industrial emissions, especially those that come from steel and cement production, are responsible for almost half of the PM2.5 pollution in the region, where more than 100 million people live (Li, et al., 2017). Aiming to cut the average PM2.5 by 25 per cent, in 2003 Beijing initiated the largest scale shutdown of steel factories in the history of the industrialized world. To combat the damage from pollution inflicted by serious episodes of toxic haze, the campaign reduced the production levels of steel, cement, and aluminium, ordered the closure of brick making and pottery factories, curtailed the number of construction projects, and placed restrictions on the operation of diesel-powered trucks. At the same time, the campaign initiated a shift from coal to gas and electricity. By 2020, and at a cost of ¥21.55 billion, the values of the health benefits accruing from the coal-to-electricity policy are estimated at ¥41.11 billion for ambient air quality and ¥18.32 billion for indoor air quality (Zhang, et al., 2019). And blue skies are becoming more common in Beijing than they have been for many years.

All of which helps to explain why Ian was so surprised to see such heavy hazes in the skies of Singapore, a city that has established itself as the greenest in Asia.

'We've been suffering from smoke hazes from time to time,' the lady explained.

'How come? Is industrial pollution that bad in Singapore?' asked Ian.

'No, the pollutants are coming from Indonesia. Singapore has been affected almost every year by severe smoke haze from forest fires occurring in many areas of Indonesia. The main reason is the long-standing common practice of farmers and agricultural landowners there to use open burning to clear forestlands for agricultural use. Prevailing winds then carry the smoke and dust in our direction, and we're very close to Indonesia,' the lady explained patiently.

Opening her backpack, she then passed Ian a mask, saying 'Here, you'll need this! The haze in Singapore has a strong acrid and burning smell, and it can cause irritation of eyes, nose, and throat if you stay outside for long.'

'Thank you so much' Ian responded gratefully, accepting the mask, 'I never thought I would need this in Singapore!'

Over the past two decades, most fires and haze in the ASEAN region have been caused directly by human intervention rather than by natural events (Qadri, 2001). In Indonesia, some peatlands (waterlogged areas filled with decomposing forest debris, decaying organisms, and vegetation) have been drained and cleared for oil palm plantations as well as other uses. Not only are drained peatlands highly susceptible to fires, but such fires are difficult to extinguish because they can smoulder as deep as three metres underground. This is especially so during the dry El Niño seasons. While the burning-related air pollution is caused mostly by local sources of emissions, it is difficult to contain hazes within the source locations. Therefore, transboundary haze from Indonesia periodically chokes its next-door neighbours, Singapore and Malaysia.

The 1997 heat haze event experienced by Singapore, when the twenty-four-hour Pollution Standard Index (PSI) reached the 'unhealthy' level of 138, was the first to receive international attention. During the event of 2013, a new record was set when the three-hour PSI reached 401, which is considerably higher than the threshold set for the 'hazardous' level (Sheldon and Sankaran, 2017). The haze causes irritation to eyes and, when inhaled for prolonged periods, can have harmful long-term effects on the lungs, heart, and respiratory system (Jayachandran, 2009). In Singapore, the fluctuations of air pollutants are somewhat dependent on local economic activities and seasonal changes but are highly correlated with the forest fires in neighbouring Indonesia (Agarwal, et al., 2020).

When Ian became quiet, the lady consoled him by saying, 'Don't be so sad! The haze is very unpredictable because it depends totally on wind direction and speed. Maybe it will be gone tomorrow!'

'Thank you for your kind words,' Ian replied with a grateful smile.

As soon as he stepped outside Changi Airport, Ian noticed the strong smell of burning. For the next half hour, he wore the mask on the taxi ride to the Marina Bay Sands hotel, which is Singapore's architectural icon. Standing as an unmissable fixture of Singapore's skyline, the Marina Bay Sands has been gracing almost every local postcard since its opening in 2010. From the time Ian received the first postcard from his cousin, Liz—who migrated to Singapore several years ago and is now an assistant professor at the School of Design and Environment of National University of Singapore—Ian has wanted to visit this hotel. Accordingly, he planned the trip carefully and made online reservations for his first two nights at the Marina Bay Sands hotel, before staying at Liz's home for the following two weeks.

As fatigue set in, Ian's excitement began to fade. Peering through the window of his hotel room, which was meant to offer breathtaking views of the vast Marina Bay, the enchanting Supertrees of Gardens by the Bay, and the iconic Singapore Flyer, all he could see was the haze. Despite the pleasant interiors, the impeccable cleanliness of his room, the delicious food at the bar, and the helpful and friendly staff, Ian couldn't help but feel disappointed and overcharged for the experience. Frustrated by these sentiments, he decided to express his feelings through an online survey completed on the day of his checkout.

Liz's face lit up with a warm smile as she drove up to Ian to pick him up. 'Hey! Long time no see!' she exclaimed; her voice filled with genuine delight.

'Thanks for picking me up,' Ian said gratefully as he got into the car.

'Aren't you happy to see me?' she teased playfully.

Ian shook his head and responded, 'Oh, it's not that I'm not happy to see you. It's just that the haze has dampened my spirits for the past two days. I couldn't enjoy any views from my "Harbour View" room or even from the rooftop infinity pool due to poor visibility. And to make matters worse, I constantly feel dirty after coming back inside, so I end up taking three showers a day.'

'What a coincidence!' giggled Liz. 'The experience you've had is related exactly to my recent research. Let me explain it to you! In our study, we collected around 1.7 million online reviews from popular platforms such as Booking, Trip Advisor, Agoda, and Expedia for all the hotels in Singapore and Hong Kong from 2012 to 2016. From the feedback provided in the reviews, we found that during the haze period, there was a temporary decrease of 0.409 points, which amounts to 5.2 per cent of the average review score on a 0–10 grading scale. However, after the haze subsided, there was an average increase of approximately 0.295 points for the review scores. What's more interesting and surprising is our finding that the average review score rises immediately after the haze shock by 0.502 points by the end of the second month; but the sharp rise is short-lived and seen only in the first three months following the haze shock.'

'Oh, so you find that consumers are more satisfied with the hotel service after the haze dissipates?' Ian asked.

'Yes, that's what our assessment shows. We used machine learning techniques and econometric models to analyse the sentiments expressed in the guest reviews. And our analysis showed that although the firm's productivity or service quality in the workplace is not affected at all, air pollution can negatively affect the mood of travellers. This suggests, of course, that reviews are related more to travellers' moods than to any real dissatisfaction with service levels. After the haze dissipates, managers respond more actively to negative reviews and make improvements to service quality in order to restore their reputations following pollution shocks. But in the long run, such efforts do not persist.'

Liz continued, her voice filled with conviction, 'Firms understand the importance of maintaining a positive online reputation, which serves as a driving force behind their commitment to delivering exceptional service. However, it's worth noting that many companies, despite having the capacity to improve their service quality, still operate below their optimal level.'

Ian blinked in surprise, intrigued by Liz's perspective. 'Really? That's very interesting! But it also seems that negative events can unexpectedly pave the way for positive outcomes.'

Excitedly, Liz nodded. Eventually, they reached her house. Liz parked the car and gestured for Ian to follow her inside. Liz wasted no time as they stepped into her home, making her way swiftly to her desk where she eagerly opened her computer. She presented figures 3.1 and 3.2 on the screen.

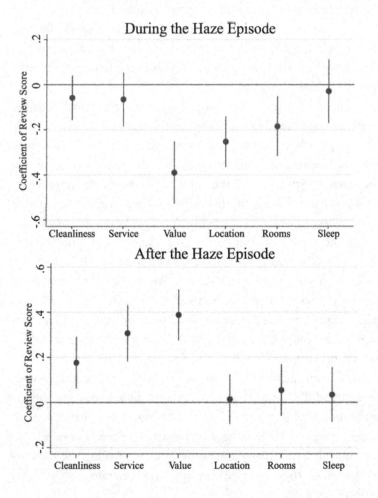

Figure 3.1: Estimated effects on sub-category reviews

Source: Agarwal, S., Wang, L., & Yang, Y. (2021). Impact of transboundary air pollution on service quality and consumer satisfaction. *Journal of Economic Behavior & Organization, 192,* 357–380.
Note: This figure plots the pollution effects on consumers' responses in each subcategory of reviews during (top) and after (bottom) the haze shock.

'We use the scores of "improvable" aspects, such as cleanliness and service, to measure service quality of hotels, and use the scores of "non-improvable" aspects, such as experience, location, and room, to measure the objective aspects of the stay experience.' Liz added, 'The top graph shows the effect during the haze and the bottom one shows the effect during a fourteen-month period after the haze.'

Looking at the graph carefully, Ian concluded, 'It looks like the scores of "improvables" don't change much during the haze episodes, but the scores of "non-improvables" drop a lot! After the haze is gone, though, the scores of "improvables" jump while the other three remain the same.'

'Yes, and we also want to estimate the impacts of air pollution events on the changes of guests' subjective well-being.' Pointing to Figure 3.2, Liz explained to Ian, 'This graph shows the welfare gains and losses. The dark line indicates the entire path of dynamic response of the online review scores of hotels in Singapore to air pollution shock relative to the ex-ante benchmark review scores, using as the control group online reviews from hotels in Hong Kong. The white bar indicates the monthly total room revenue in millions of Singapore dollars. One guest per night experiences a S$15.86 welfare loss as a result of the haze shock, but travellers to Singapore enjoy on average a service improvement estimated at S$5.67 per room per night in the twelve months following a haze shock.'

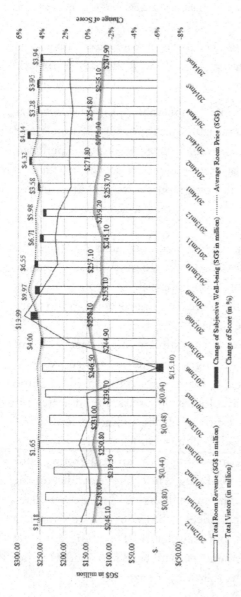

Figure 3.2: Welfare analysis

Source: This figure shows the welfare analysis based on the estimates in Agarwal, S., Wang, L., & Yang, Y. (2021). Impact of transboundary air pollution on service quality and consumer satisfaction. *Journal of Economic Behavior & Organization, 192,* 357–380.

Note: The dark line in this figure indicates the entire path of dynamic response of the online review scores of hotels in Singapore to air pollution shock relative to the ex-ante benchmark review scores, using online reviews from hotels in Hong Kong as the control group. The green line indicates the monthly arrivals of international investors. The dotted line indicates the monthly average room price of hotels in Singapore. The white bar indicates the monthly total room revenue in millions of Singapore dollars. The solid bar indicates the monthly welfare gains of losses in the form of total room revenue.

Hearing this, Ian suddenly understood why he had felt he overpaid for his stay at Marina Bay Sands.

'You should have told me earlier about your research into the Singapore haze!' Ian exclaimed, 'I could have changed the hotel booking and stayed there after the haze ended, so I could enjoy not only the beautiful view, but also the better service quality. And by the way, Liz, tomorrow I'm going to meet James, who mentioned he'll need to sign a housing deal in the morning. Do you want to go together? It could be a good opportunity to catch up and explore the city together.'

Liz smiled and replied, 'That sounds interesting! I'd be delighted to join you. Let's make it a productive and enjoyable day.'

James had been Ian's roommate in college. After working as a bank manager in Singapore for several years, he had finally decided to buy his first flat. Very pro-environment, James has been actively looking for Green Mark homes. As defined in Kollmuss and Agyeman (2002), 'pro-environment' refers to behaviour that actively seeks opportunities to minimize the negative impacts of one's actions on the natural and built world (for example, through minimizing resource and energy consumption, using non-toxic substances, and reducing waste production). It was discovered that pro-environmental behaviour can be influenced by factors that are internal to the individual person, as well as by factors that are external, or societal. Internal variables can include motives related to ecosystem health, personal health, local environmental quality, global warming, and 'warm-glow' (or intrinsic) satisfaction. External variables include such factors as household income and standard socio-demographic characteristics (Clark, et al., 2003). Early models of pro-environmental behaviour in the 1970s were based on the concept of a linear progression of environmental knowledge that would lead to environmental awareness and concern (environmental attitudes), which in turn was expected to lead to pro-environmental behaviour. But research showed this model to be flawed, since increased awareness had not in fact led to pro-environmental behaviour (Owens, 2000).

Placing high emphasis on environmental sustainability in its pursuit of economic growth, Singapore has become recognized as a green and clean city. To promote the construction of energy efficient and environmentally friendly buildings in Singapore, the Building and Construction Authority (BCA) launched the Green Mark Scheme in January 2005. In awarding the Green Mark label, the BCA is identifying buildings that incorporate internationally recognized practices in energy performance and environmental design. By evaluating the environmental impact and performance of a building, the Green Mark provides a framework for assessing and differentiating both new and existing buildings in the real estate market. It is marketed as an instrument for achieving reductions in water and energy consumption, improving indoor environmental quality, and mitigating potential environmental risks. And, equally importantly, the Green Mark recognizes the strong commitment of some developers to social responsibility and environmental sustainability.

Depending on the assessment criteria that evaluate energy and water efficiency, environmental protection, indoor quality, and other green features, as well as innovation, a building can be certified at one of four rating levels: BCA Green Mark Platinum, GoldPlus, Gold, and Certified. Developers, building owners, and government agencies can follow a BCA procedure to assess buildings against the certification criteria. Under existing building criteria, a re-assessment is required every three years. Furthermore, the certification standards are updated every two years to reflect technological progress in the building industry.

Not only has Singapore's progress to date in the 'greening' of the construction industry been impressive, but the BCA's goal is to achieve green certification of at least 80 per cent of buildings by 2030, and thereby become a global leader in the area of green construction with expertise in tropical and sub-tropical environments. The Green Mark covers the commercial, residential, retail, industry, hotel, institutional, office, park, and public housing sectors, with codes and regulations that differ between residential and non-residential buildings.

Furthermore, to help accelerate the rate of growth of green construction in Singapore, the government has created funding and incentive schemes that support the adoption of an integrated design, green building technologies, and environment-friendly construction practices. By way of contrast, funding for green construction programmes in the US is constrained by limited cash incentives (Kingsley, 2008). In fact, only 54 cities (2.7 per cent of the US population) can make use of the density bonus incentive. Developers in Singapore have access to many more funding programmes than US developers. In Singapore, the incentive schemes are targeted mainly at private sector projects, especially those that have achieved the BCA Green Mark Gold rating or higher.

The next morning, Ian, Liz, and James had a traditional Singaporean breakfast of soft-cooked eggs with kaya jam and toast, as well as Koppi-C (coffee with sugar and evaporated milk). With skies hazy across the city, they went to Greenway Sunrise, a residential project that was awarded a GoldPlus label by BCA Singapore.

Enthusiastically, James exclaimed to Ian and Liz, 'You know, I've always wanted to live in a green building!' He eagerly pointed out the key features listed on the advertising brochure, which were indeed eye-catching: estimated energy savings of 1,009,816 kWh/year and estimated water savings of 29,224 m3/year. However, Liz remained unconvinced.

Drawing attention to the pollution by clearing her throat with a noisy 'Ahem,' Liz observed, 'The haze is getting worse!' She then turned to James and, looking at him seriously, said, 'Ask the seller to give you a better price!'

James's eyes popped wide open with surprise, 'How?'

'Two points, James.' Liz pointed to the hazy sky, 'First, buyers could be worse off by paying a higher price if they negotiate housing deals on a polluted day. Let me tell you why.

Because the buyers are at the last stage of buying a house, they've already made the decision to work and live in the particular city. This means their only choices are to stay in their current residence, or to buy the house and move to another residence in the same city. Air pollution causes the same negative shock to both their current living quality and their potential future living quality. However, although the absolute difference between potential future living quality and current living quality stays unchanged, the proportional improvement in living quality over the current one actually increases on polluted days. If we represent living quality in numerical values, we might say for example that buyers' current living quality is 100, whereas the new house provides a living quality of 150. Therefore, the absolute increase in living quality is 50, and the proportional increase is $50/100 = 50$ per cent. With air pollution negatively influencing living qualities (e.g. -20), the absolute difference is still 50, but the proportional increase is now $50/(100–20) = 62.5$ per cent. Due to relative thinking, buyers tend to consider a 62.5 per cent increase more attractive than a 50 per cent increase and are thus willing to pay a higher price for this improvement,' she explained.

This phenomenon is reflected in research (Qin et al., 2019) showing that in Beijing, all else being equal, transaction prices on a severely polluted day are 0.65 per cent higher than those on the days without pollution. The difference translates into approximately a ¥3.51 million daily increase, based on the average transaction volume and price on a typical day in Beijing. Non-local and low-income buyers are the main drivers of this effect, which can be explained by what is called the 'salience thinking' of home buyers (Bordalo et al., 2012, 2013a, 2013b). When considering different living alternatives, the buyer's attention is drawn more strongly to living quality by its larger relative change due to pollution; thus, price becomes less salient. Consequently, on a polluted day, buyers would be more likely to accept a higher price in the price negotiation, which then leads to a higher probability of a deal if the sellers do not change their behaviour according to air pollution levels.

'Second,' continued Liz, 'Do you really believe that green buildings are "greener"? Because this may not be true.'

'I know that buildings with green labels are generally more expensive in China,' said Ian.

'Yes, and it is the same case in Singapore, the US, the UK, and many other countries.' Liz said, 'Buyers pay premiums for green buildings.'

Greater marketing opportunities and enhanced building performance are the primary motivators for building green (Matisoff, Noonan, and Flowers, 2016). Consumers who believe in the cost-effectiveness of green buildings, place a high value on green certification and are willing to pay a premium for green features. And indeed, research focusing on green certification in the commercial market supports a positive relationship between green labels and property prices (Eichholtz, Kok, and Quigley, 2010, 2013; Devine and Kok, 2015; Deng, Li, and Quigley, 2012). For example, Walls et al. (2017) analyse housing transactions in the urban areas in the US and find the Energy Star Certification is associated with 2 per cent price premium. Chegut, Eichholtz, and Kok (2014) state that the development of green buildings in the UK increases the value of nearby conventional buildings, pointing to positive externalities from green certification. However, while existing studies provide evidence for the existence of green premiums in the residential sector (Kahn and

Kok, 2014; Ramos, et al., 2015; Fuerst, et al., 2015; Chegut, Eichholtz, and Holtermans, 2016; Walls, et al., 2017), the reasons for such premiums remain unclear.

'So, do you know why buyers pay more for green buildings?' Liz continued. 'First, the green mark certification sends a positive message about the overall quality of buildings and the reputation of developers, thereby increasing market values. Second, energy-efficient facilities in green mark buildings are expected to reduce future energy costs. The estimated cost savings translate into higher prices for green buildings, and consumers like you are willing to pay more.'

'Yes, I do believe that I can save a lot by living in a green building. And along with the energy savings, I'm willing to pay the premium for better building quality and positive image,' said James. Then he added, 'Em, wait though, do you know how much the premium is?'

'In Singapore, green dwellings are 4.2 per cent more expensive than comparable non-certified dwellings, and in the US, the green premium is around 2.1 per cent,' answered Liz, 'so the question here is whether it's worthwhile to pay the 4.2 per cent premium for the expected energy savings.'

To assess the energy efficiency of buildings, much US research uses cross-sectional data of the source energy consumption or site energy consumption data. This data is reported at the time of building design for green building certification in accordance with Leadership in Energy and Environmental Design (LEED) requirements. Newsham et al. (2009) conducted an analysis of commercial green buildings in the United States using the simulated energy performance data of 100 medium-energy, LEED-certified commercial and institutional buildings in the United States. Based on various matching criteria, such as activity type, size, age, and climate zone, the study paired each LEED building with a very similar conventional commercial building, and found that on average, LEED commercial buildings, on average, used 18–39 per cent less energy per floor area than their conventional counterparts. Nevertheless, the paper identifies that a notable portion of LEED buildings (approximately 28–35 per cent) exhibited higher energy consumption compared to their conventional counterparts. In addition, the study shows little correlation between the simulated energy performance of the buildings and their certification level. Similarly, using the gross floor space (GFS) weighted source energy data of 121 LEED buildings in the United States, Scofield (2009) found that LEED-certified commercial buildings show no significant primary energy savings over comparable non-LEED buildings on average.

Liz said, 'We've studied this question in one of our research projects. Taking all the residential buildings in Singapore, we found no significant differences in energy consumptions between Green Mark certified buildings and conventional buildings. In fact, we found that when the buildings operate at the full load during the days, green buildings consume 4.39 per cent more electricity, on average, than conventional buildings. This can be explained by a plausible rebound effect of increased energy consumption when residents know their buildings are labelled "energy efficient". So, without the expected energy savings, green housing may not be worth the premium price.'

'Em, it's really useful to know all this! I know how to haggle, so I'll handle it from here,' nodded James. 'Hey Liz, I really learnt a lot from you!'

'I learn from her every day,' laughed Ian.

Chapter 4

The Invisible Cost of Air Pollution: What About Productivity?

After learning about the negative impact of air pollution on consumer satisfaction in the hospitality industry, Ian became intrigued by the topic and decided to investigate further. As an avid traveller and environmental enthusiast, he was interested in learning how air pollution was affecting the travel industry. Ian set his sights on Ctrip, China's largest travel agency. Ctrip is mainly involved in arranging travel for its clients and generates revenue through commissions from hotels, airlines, and tour operators. The company was listed on the NASDAQ stock exchange in 2003 and had a market capitalization of over $25 billion at the end of 2022.

Ian had set his sights on visiting one of their call centres, faced with the choice between Nantong and Shanghai. After careful consideration, he decided to explore the centre in Nantong. Upon arrival, he was immediately struck by the impressive scale and size of the operation. Nestled within a spacious and climate-controlled building, the call centre boasted modern telecommunications and computing hardware, reflecting the organization's commitment to staying up to date with technological advancements.

As Ian entered the call centre, he was greeted by the manager, Mr Yang, who showed him around the facilities. As they walked through the rows of cubicles, Ian noticed that each worker had a computer and a phone headset. The workers followed identical staffing practices and procedural guidelines, with a central server that automatically routed customer calls and assignments to workers based on a computerized call-queuing system. 'I'm interested in learning more about how your workers are compensated,' Ian said. 'Can you tell me more about that?'

'Of course,' Mr Yang replied. 'All of our workers receive compensation based on their productivity, which is primarily determined by call and order volumes. We also make adjustments for call quality. We keep track of various measures of on-the-job performance for each worker to determine their productivity level.'

'I see,' Ian said. 'How do workers feel about this system? Does it create any kind of competition or tension between them?'

Mr Yang explained, 'Actually, our workers are very motivated by the productivity-based pay system. It encourages them to work harder and take on more calls, which helps us meet our goals and provide better service to our customers. We also have training programmes to help workers improve their productivity and earn higher pay.'

'That's interesting,' Ian said. 'Have you noticed any trends in terms of which workers tend to be the most productive?'

Mr Yang thought for a moment before replying, 'It varies from person to person, but usually, workers who are able to maintain a high level of focus and concentration throughout the day tend to be the most productive. We also find that workers who take advantage of our training programmes and use the tools we provide tend to be more productive as well.'

Mr Yang continued the tour, 'We just upgraded the building with air purifiers and fresh air ventilation systems,' the manager said, gesturing towards the machines. 'It's part of our efforts to improve the productivity and well-being of our workers.'

Ian was intrigued. 'That's interesting. Have you noticed any improvements since installing the air purifiers?'

Mr Yang nodded. 'Yes, we have. We actually collaborated with a group of researchers in the US to conduct a study on the impact of pollution on worker productivity. The study found that pollution has a significant negative effect on worker productivity, and that air purifiers can help mitigate this effect.'

Ian recognized the study the manager was referring to. 'You're talking about the study by Chang, Graff Zivin, Gross, and Neidell, right? It is the first study that investigates the impact of air pollution on workers whose primary jobs require cognitive ability rather than physical performance.'

Mr Yang smiled. 'Yes, that's the one. It's great to see that you're familiar with it. The study investigates how changes in the air quality index, especially fine particulate matter, affect worker productivity.'

Panel A. Shanghai (Total: 589 workdays)

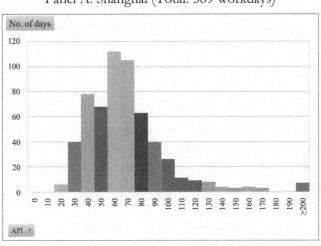

Panel B. Nantong (Total: 189 workdays)

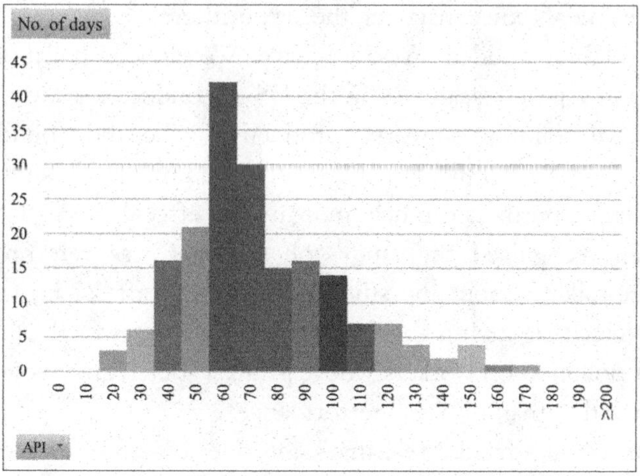

Figure 4.1: Histograms of pollution in Shanghai and Nantong

Source: Chang, T. Y., Graff Zivin, J., Gross, T., and Neidell, M. (2019). 'The effect of pollution on worker productivity: evidence from call center workers in China.' *American Economic Journal: Applied Economics*, 11(1), 151–72.
Note: These figures present the distribution of API observed on workdays in Nantong and Shanghai in the data of Chang et al. (2019).

In China, the Air Quality Index (API)—a composite score that evaluates air quality based on its associated health risks—is determined by combining concentrations of three criteria air pollutants into a single index, using a formula developed by the US EPA. Specifically, the API is determined by calculating the maximum value of a nonlinear transformation of three pollutants: PM10, NO_2, and SO_2. The API is a cardinal index, with higher values indicating worse air quality. API values below 100 are considered safe for most people, while those between 100 and 150 are labelled as potentially harmful for vulnerable individuals. Levels exceeding 150 can have significant adverse effects on the overall population. Throughout the study conducted by Chang et al. (2019), for API levels higher than 50, PM10 was the dominant pollutant over 99 per cent of the time.

'Fine particulate matter? why it is important to focus on that?' asked Ian.

Mr Yang explained, 'You know, recent research has shown something quite interesting. It suggests that exposure to fine particulate matter, those tiny particles in the air, can actually have a negative impact on our cognitive abilities and brain performance. These particles, because of their small size, can enter our bloodstream and make their way to our central nervous system, even deep within the brain stem. And when that happens, it can trigger inflammation, cortical stress, and damage to our blood vessels. As a result, our intelligence and performance in cognitive tasks may decrease.'

Multiple studies have demonstrated the detrimental effects of exposure to fine particulate matter on brain health (Suglia et al., 2008; Power et al., 2011; Weuve et al., 2012; and Peters et al., 2006). The manager continued, 'There have been several studies supporting these findings. For example, in a study conducted by Ebenstein, Lavy, and Roth, they found a strong association between high levels of these particles and worse performance on important exams. It's quite concerning, isn't it?'

As Ian and Mr Yang continued their tour, the manager explained to Ian why the call centre workers were chosen for the study. 'Our call centre workers are ideal subjects for the study because they have little discretion over their labour supply,' the manager said. 'This means that we can accurately measure the effects of pollution on productivity without worrying about any changes in labour composition. For instance, if only the most productive workers come to work on polluted days, we would underestimate the productivity effects of pollution.'

Mr Yang went on to explain further. 'Additionally, daily variations in pollution levels in Shanghai and Nantong are likely unrelated to our firm's output. We serve clients throughout China, and demand for our services on any given day is probably not affected by local pollution levels. Furthermore, because calls are randomly routed to the two call centres, we can directly test whether any correlation between pollution and productivity is driving our results.'

Ian nodded, impressed with the thoroughness of the study design. 'It seems like the research team thought of everything,' he remarked.

However, he wondered if traffic could have been a factor that biased the results because commuting to work in Shanghai was known to be tiring and stressful.

Mr Yang smiled and said, 'That's a valid concern. A randomized experiment was conducted at Ctrip allowed the research team to examine the influence of traffic as a potential confounder.'

Traffic can be a crucial variable that affects worker productivity as it not only causes pollution but also emotional stress and tardiness. A survey conducted by Statista in 2015 found that residents of Shanghai, on average, spent approximately fifty-one minutes travelling to work during their daily commute. To account for the impact of traffic, a randomized experiment was conducted where a portion of the employees were allowed to work from home during the study period. This experiment was designed to assess the significance of traffic in the study's findings.

'Can you tell me more about the experiment?' Ian was curious.

'Approximately 250 employees from the Shanghai office worked from home during part of our study period, with a comparably sized control group,' Mr Yang explained. 'The experiment ran from 6 December 2010 until 14 August 2011, during which time the home-based workers were provided with the necessary equipment to allow them to perform their usual work responsibilities in a manner identical to that at the office.'

'So, what you're saying is that you conducted an experiment to analyse the impact of pollution on workers who worked from home compared to those who worked in the office?' Ian asked.

'Yes, it was a significant undertaking, but it allowed us to get a better understanding of the effects of traffic on worker productivity,' the manager replied. 'Traffic is a potentially important confounder because it generates pollution and can directly reduce productivity by both creating emotional stress and making employees late for work.'

Ian nodded and his curiosity piqued. He asked Mr Yang, 'Regarding the experiment, what were the findings related to pollution?'

'Well, we found that pollution had a negative impact on the number of phone calls taken by workers who worked both from the office and at home,' Mr Yang explained.

Chang et al. (2019) unveil a considerable negative impact of air pollution on employee productivity. Precisely, the study discovered that each 10-unit rise in the API caused a reduction in worker productivity, as determined by the number of daily calls handled, by an average of 0.35 per cent. The statistical analysis shows that as pollution levels increase, there is a gradual and steady decline in productivity among workers, and this trend is more evident as the API reaches levels above 100 for certain productivity measures and above 150 for all of them. The study also discovered that the reduction in the number of calls made by workers was due to an increase in the duration of breaks taken, rather than changes in the length of the phone calls themselves.

'But wait, what about traffic?' Ian asked.

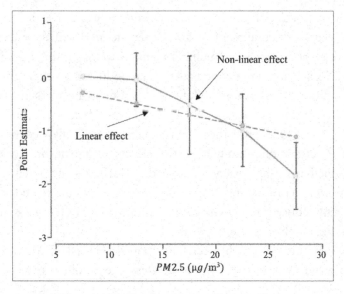

Figure 4.2: Linear and non-linear effects
of PM2.5 on productivity

Source: Chang, T.Y., Graff Zivin, J., Gross, T., and Neidell, M. (2019). 'The effect of pollution on worker productivity: evidence from call center workers in China.' *American Economic Journal: Applied Economics*, 11(1), 151–72.

Mr Yang shook his head. 'The results suggest that traffic is not a significant factor when it comes to the impact of pollution on worker productivity. Researchers compared the workers who worked at home to those who worked in the office and found that their productivity levels were similar, even though those who worked from home didn't have to deal with a daily commute. This means that traffic is unlikely to be a source of confounding for the productivity effects that we observed.'

Ian followed Mr Yang to his office. He warmly thanked Mr Yang for opening his eyes to the research on fine particulate matter. They took their seats and settled in, ready to delve deeper into the fascinating topic at hand. 'It's important for us to be aware of the impact of pollution on our workers. It's always good to stay informed about these things, especially since air pollution affects so many people,' Mr Yang said.

Ian asked, 'What other impacts can pollution have on workers besides those in office buildings?'

Mr Yang replied, 'Well, I've learned from the research team in the US that they also studied the impact of air pollution on workers in the agriculture sector.'

Ian was intrigued and asked, 'Oh, really? Please tell me more!'

'The experimental study has been carried out at a large fruit farm located at the Central Valley in California,' Mr Yang explained. 'The study focuses on the daily productivity of the agricultural workers at the fruit farm and investigates the impact of ozone on the productivity of these workers. Workers involved in the study sample are paid through piece rate contracts, so their daily earnings are directly linked to the amount of work they complete. The research found that when ozone levels were high, worker productivity decreased significantly, resulting in lower earnings. This is concerning for both the workers and the company, as it suggests that air pollution can have a direct impact on productivity and profits.'

'The regional transport of NOx from Los Angeles and San Francisco has imposed a tremendous impact on the ozone level in Central Valley,' Mr Yang continued. 'Since there are limited local sources of ozone in the vicinity, emissions of nitrogen oxides and volatile organic chemicals from distant urban activities are likely to be the major contributors of ozone in the region. This means that the air quality in the Central Valley is heavily influenced by factors outside of our control, which makes it all the more important for the study to monitor and understand the impacts of air pollution on our workers and our business.'

Ozone pollution has been a long-standing environmental concern in many countries. Instead of being directly emitted into the air, ozone is formed through complex interactions between nitrogen oxides (NOx) and volatile organic chemicals (VOCs) that are emitted directly. These reactions are influenced by sunlight and heat, causing ozone levels and daily environmental conditions to fluctuate with temperature changes. Exposure to ozone can have harmful effects on respiratory health, including irritation of the lung airways, decreased lung function, and respiratory symptoms (Neidell, 2009). This can be particularly problematic for people who work in physically demanding jobs, such as agriculture, where decreased lung function can negatively impact productivity. However, once individuals are no longer exposed to ozone, their lung function typically recovers quickly. In fact, most healthy adults can expect to see their lung function return to baseline levels within twenty-four hours of exposure.

Mr Yang adjusted his glasses and pulled out a report. 'Well, there were a few key findings,' he began. 'First, agricultural workers are typically exposed to considerably higher levels of air pollution than individuals who work indoors.'

Ian nodded. 'That's not surprising, what else did they discover? What about worker behaviour in response to ozone levels?'

'When ozone levels fall well below the federal air quality standards, it exerts a significant impact on productivity,' Mr Yang continued. 'A decrease of 10 parts per billion (ppb) in ozone exposure would result in a robust increase in worker productivity by 5.5 per cent in the agricultural context.'

Mr Yang flipped through the report. 'Interestingly, the number of hours worked is not significantly related to ozone levels, meaning that the farm workers did not perform regular adjustments to their work schedules in response to ozone levels. This indicates the absence of avoidance behaviour. However, pollution will indirectly increase workers' incentive of work-shirking.'

Ian scratched his head. 'Hmm, that's something to consider. And what about the financial impact of reducing ozone levels?'

Mr Yang smiled. 'A back-of-the-envelope calculation applying the estimated environmental productivity effect in the Central Valley to the whole United States suggested that a 10-ppb reduction in the ozone standard, which is currently being considered by the US EPA, could be conveyed into an annual cost saving in labour-related expenditures of approximately $700 million.'

Ian whistled. 'That's quite a savings. And what about other countries?'

'Ah yes,' Mr Yang said, turning to another section of the report. 'In developing countries that depend more heavily on agriculture for their national incomes, the ozone-induced productivity effects are more likely to have considerable impacts on the well-being of households and the nationwide economy. The negative impacts of ozone may be particularly severe in countries like India, China, and Mexico, which exhibit skyrocketing growth in the manufacturing sector and automobile penetration. These activities would rapidly produce the antecedent chemical components for ozone formation and would hence result in substantially higher levels of ozone pollution.'

Ian frowned. 'That's not good news. Were there any notable differences or variations in how ozone affected individuals based on factors like age, gender, or experience?'

Mr Yang nodded. 'Interestingly, there is no evidence supporting that more experienced workers would have a higher resilience to ozone for having a better ability in setting an optimal working pace throughout the day. However, it has been observed that ozone has a smaller impact on productivity for women, though the marginal difference between men and women is quite small.'

As he shuffled through the report, Mr Yang continued, 'Moreover, the research indicates that workers involved in job tasks with higher physical demands are more likely to suffer from lung functioning impairments due to air pollution. This effect is especially pronounced when workers engage in vigorous exercise, such as the physical demands required for blueberry harvesting.'

Ian nodded, absorbing the information. 'So, what can we do about it?'

'We need to take action to reduce air pollution levels in our workplace,' Mr Yang said firmly. 'According to this report, the impacts of ozone on workers' lung functioning begin to emerge at levels as low as 42–46 ppb. That's well below the current air quality standard of 75 ppb, and even lower than the proposed reforms of the current standard, which would be at 60 ppb.'

Ian's mind raced as he considered the implications. 'So, if we don't take action, our workers could be experiencing reduced lung functioning and impaired productivity without even realizing it.'

'By implementing stronger regulations on ozone pollution, we can not only improve public health, but also enhance worker productivity,' Mr Yang explained.

Ian was deep in thought. Suddenly, he had another question. 'What about PM2.5? Could that have the same negative impact as ozone on labour productivity?'

Mr Yang nodded. 'That's a good question. In fact, there has been some research on that very topic.'

He shuffled through some papers on his desk and pulled out another report. 'This study looked at the productivity of pear packers and the effects of particulate pollution. It found that exposure to PM2.5 had a significant negative impact on their productivity.'

Although exposure to lower levels of PM2.5 can cause subtle health effects such as mild headaches, changes in blood pressure, and irritation in the ear, nose, and throat, these effects are usually overlooked by econometricians since they generally do not lead to healthcare encounters and may even go unnoticed by the affected individuals. Therefore, the actual impact of pollution on work productivity may be underestimated.

Mr Yang went on to explain the study, 'The researchers in the US conducted an experimental study at the largest pear-packing factory in Northern California, which is located near a weather and pollution station just 2.7 miles away. The aim of the study was to examine the productivity of workers during their regular day shifts and measure it on a daily basis. To determine how productive the workers were, the researchers used a standardized measure of productivity which was based on each worker's total earnings per hour for all types of packaging they were doing.'

Chang et al. (2016) revealed a statistically significant negative impact of PM2.5 pollution on the marginal productivity of manufacturing workers working indoors and that the negative effect would occur when the pollution levels got well below the US National Ambient Air Quality Standards (NAAQS). An increase in PM2.5 pollution of 10 micrograms per cubic metre (μg/m3) would reduce the productivity of workers by $0.41 per hour, which is approximately a 6 per cent decrease of the average hourly earnings without the negative influence brought by particulate pollution. Such negative effects begin to arise once the PM2.5 concentration exceeds 15 μg/m3.

Ian listened carefully as Mr Yang continued. 'According to their estimations, the decrease in PM2.5 has brought aggregated savings in labour costs for around $19.5 billion, which represents a 2.67 per cent increase of earnings in the manufacturing sector, as well as a 0.5 per cent increase in economy-wide earnings. From 1999 to 2008, the total reductions in PM2.5 has saved approximately $19.5 billion labour related costs. Lastly, the majority of PM2.5 output among the richest nations are produced indoors.'

Ian nodded thoughtfully as Mr Yang finished explaining the study's results. 'This study seems to have significant implications for both workers and businesses,' he remarked. 'So, if I understand correctly, even a moderate exposure to PM2.5 can lead to subtle but economically relevant reductions in labour productivity?'

'Exactly,' replied Mr Yang. 'And these effects could potentially impact a significant fraction of the nation's economy. That's why it's crucial to look at the broader context and understand the macroscopic effects of PM2.5.'

Ian furrowed his brow. 'So, other jobs with similar physical requirements to pear packers are also likely to be negatively affected by PM2.5?'

'Yes,' confirmed Mr Yang. 'The study's findings suggest that workers in other occupations that require similar physical exertion could be impacted in a similar way.'

Ian nodded in agreement. 'It's also interesting to note that traditional methods for assessing workers' welfare often fail to take health problems caused by air and particulate pollution into account. This could result in substantial underestimation of the benefits of environmental quality improvements.'

'Exactly,' said Mr Yang. 'Reducing pollution can be viewed as an investment in human capital that promotes firm productivity and economic growth. As part of our commitment to our employees' well-being, we have taken steps to ensure proper ventilation and air filtration systems in our call centres. We also provide our workers with protective masks and encourage them to take regular breaks to get fresh air outside. It's important to prioritize the health and productivity of our workforce.'

Ian nodded, 'Businesses and policymakers should realize the importance of public policy in shaping outcomes in the area of pollution control. And public policy plays a critical role in shaping outcomes in the area of pollution control. In fact, productivity-enhancing investments would be more efficient through publicly coordinated reductions in contamination rather than unilateral efforts by firms.'

After thanking Mr Yang for sharing the findings of the studies, Ian left the office with a newly acquired understanding of the paramount importance of safeguarding workers from the detrimental effects of pollution. The information provided by Mr Yang shed light on the need for corporate commitment to pollution control measures in order to enhance worker productivity, as well as the imperative for stronger public policies to regulate and reduce air pollution. As Ian exited the building, he felt a sense of duty to raise awareness and promote the safeguarding of workers' health and well-being amidst environmental pollution.

Chapter 5

Air Pollution Regulations:
The Manufacturing Industry's Response

Ian had witnessed firsthand the rapid development of China's economy and was acutely aware of the significant environmental challenges that came with it. When he visited his old friend Ronny, who was now a professor at ShanghaiTech University in Pudong, he hoped to learn more about the latest developments in China's carbon reduction efforts.

As he arrived at ShanghaiTech, Ian was struck by the modernity and innovation of the campus. The university was at the forefront of research and development in many fields, including sustainable technology and environmental science. He knew that Ronny and his colleagues were among the brightest minds in the city and that they were deeply committed to finding solutions to China's environmental challenges.

Ian walked into Ronny's office and greeted his old friend warmly. The two caught up on old times for a few minutes before Ronny's colleague, Professor Chen, entered the room.

After introductions were made, Professor Chen joined in the conversation about China's carbon reduction efforts. She spoke passionately about the government's initiatives and policies aimed at reducing carbon emissions and promoting sustainability. Ian was impressed by her knowledge and expertise in the field.

SO$_2$

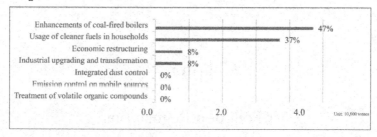

NO$_x$

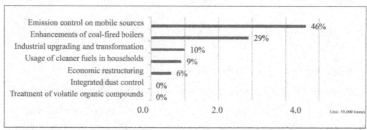

VOCs

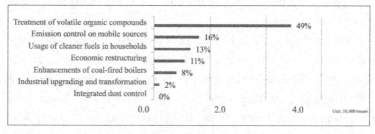

PM$_{2.5}$

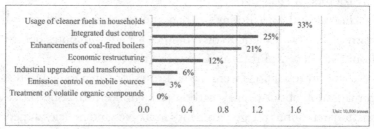

Figure 5.1: Contribution of various mitigation measures
in reducing emissions of the major pollutants in Beijing
between 2013 and 2017

Source: Cheng, J., Su, J., Cui, T., Li, X., Dong, X., Sun, F., . . . & He, K. (2019). Dominant role of emission reduction in PM 2.5 air quality improvement in Beijing during 2013–2017: a model-based decomposition analysis. *Atmospheric Chemistry and Physics*, 19(9), 6125–6146.

'In 2020 alone, our energy consumption per unit of GDP decreased by nearly 4 per cent, and our non-fossil fuel energy consumption increased by nearly 5 per cent,' Professor Chen said. 'I'm excited to say that China has set an ambitious target to achieve carbon neutrality by 2060.' Professor Chen said.

Ian was amazed. 'That's a huge target,' he said. 'What specific policies and initiatives have been put in place to achieve these reductions?'

Professor Chen listed several examples. 'The government has implemented policies such as carbon pricing, emissions trading schemes, and subsidies for renewable energy development. We're also promoting sustainable transportation and land use, such as green buildings and sustainable urban development.'

Ronny chimed in. 'And it's not just the government that's involved. We're seeing more and more businesses and industries taking voluntary action to reduce their carbon footprint. For example, some companies are setting their own carbon reduction targets and investing in renewable energy.'

Ian was curious about the timeline for achieving carbon neutrality. 'What are the specific targets and milestones that China has set for itself?'

Professor Chen then outlined a set of goals for the future. By 2030, the aim is to achieve significant advancements in several key areas that will contribute to a more sustainable and environmentally friendly society.

One of the primary objectives is to reduce carbon emissions per unit of GDP by 65 per cent from the 2005 level. This target reflects the commitment to decouple economic growth from carbon-intensive activities and emphasizes the importance of adopting cleaner and more efficient technologies.

Additionally, there is a focus on increasing the share of non-fossil fuels in primary energy consumption to around 25 per cent by 2030. This transition to renewable energy sources, such as solar, wind, and hydro power, plays a vital role in reducing reliance on fossil fuels and mitigating greenhouse gas emissions.

Another significant aspect of the sustainability efforts is the preservation and expansion of forest resources. The goal is to increase the volume of forest stock by six billion cubic metres from the 2005 level. Forests are critical for carbon sequestration, biodiversity conservation, and providing numerous benefits to local communities.

Ronny added, 'And by 2060, our ultimate goal is to achieve carbon neutrality. It is a challenging goal, but we believe it's necessary for the future of our planet.'

Table 5.1: Identifying the three main scopes of carbon emissions as prerequisite for designing mitigation measures.

Scope of emissions	Definition	Activities defined under the Greenhouse Gas Protocol
Scope 1	Direct Emissions of Greenhouse Gases • Greenhouse gases directly emitted through fossil fuel combustion from corporates	• Self-owned boiler • Self-owned vehicles • Self-owned furnace • Chemical Production

Scope 2	Indirect emission of greenhouse gases • Greenhouse gases emitted from electricity, heating and cooling processes handled by other companies and paid for by the direct corporate	• Purchased electricity • Purchased heating • Purchased steaming • Purchased cooling
Scope 3	Other indirect emissions • Indirect emissions caused by business operations, including upstream and downstream emissions besides those defined in Scope 1 and Scope 2	• Outsourced goods and services • Capital goods • Fuel and energy related activities • Upstream transportation and distribution • Waste generated from operations • Business trips • Employee commuting • Upstream rental assets • Downstream shipping and sorting • Processing of goods sold • Utilization of goods sold • Disposal of goods sold • Downstream rental assets • Franchise • Investments

Professor Chen looked thoughtful. 'There will certainly be challenges, both technical and political,' she said. 'But we are committed to finding solutions and working with the international community to address the global challenge of climate change.'

Ronny nodded in agreement. 'It's exciting to be a part of a community that is actively engaged in finding solutions to some of the most pressing environmental challenges of our time.' Ronny turned back to Ian, 'You know, we're actually planning on visiting an aluminium factory tomorrow at the Hangzhou Bay Industrial Zone. We were invited by some of our colleagues to see firsthand the efforts being made in the industry towards carbon reduction and sustainability.'

Professor Chen nodded in agreement. 'Yes, it's a great opportunity to witness the challenges and complexities involved in reducing carbon emissions in heavy industry.'

Ian's eyes sparkled with excitement as he heard the invitation. 'Wow, that sounds absolutely amazing! I've actually been hearing a lot about the industrial park lately, and I must say, I'm pretty intrigued. Count me in! I'd love to join you and dive deeper into the practical side of these carbon reduction initiatives. It's always fascinating to see how these ideas come to life in real-world applications.'

Industrial zones, also known as economic development zones, have played a crucial role in China's economic growth over the past few decades. As of 2020, there were over 4,000 industrial zones in China (National Bureau of Statistics, 2020). These zones vary in size and location, ranging from the Suzhou Industrial Park in the east to the Shenzhen Special Economic Zone in the south.

These industrial zones have been instrumental in driving China's economic growth, with the industrial sector accounting for over 27 per cent of China's GDP in 2020 (National Bureau of Statistics, 2021). They have also been key to attracting foreign investment, with China ranking as the second-largest recipient of foreign direct investment (FDI) in the world in 2020, after the United States (United Nations Conference on Trade and Development, 2021).

However, industrial zones have also been a major source of pollution and environmental degradation in China. A 2016 report by the World Bank estimated that air and water pollution cost China the equivalent of 10 per cent of its GDP in 2013 (World Bank, 2016). The use of coal as a primary source of energy has been a major contributor to air pollution, with China being the world's largest consumer and producer of coal.

The Chinese government has stepped up its efforts to enforce environmental regulations in industrial zones. In 2019, the Ministry of Ecology and Environment carried out nationwide environmental inspections, which led to the punishment of thousands of polluting companies (Ministry of Ecology and Environment, 2019). The Ministry of Ecology and Environment also publishes an annual report on the state of the environment in China, which provides an overview of China's environmental performance and identifies areas for improvement.

Ian left Ronny's office feeling energized by the prospect of seeing China's carbon neutrality efforts in action. The following morning, he met up with Ronny and Professor Chen at ShanghaiTech University to begin their trip to the aluminium factory in Hangzhou Bay Industrial Zone.

The Hangzhou Bay Industrial Zone, located in the Shanghai–Hangzhou–Ningbo region, is one of China's largest and most advanced manufacturing hubs. With its strategic location, modern infrastructure, and a highly skilled workforce, it has attracted many multinational corporations and domestic companies, making it a vital contributor to the country's economic growth. However, the rapid industrialization has also brought significant environmental challenges, such as air and water pollution, soil contamination, and ecological degradation. The government and the industries in the zone have recognized the need for sustainable development and are taking various measures to address these issues, including implementing strict regulations, adopting clean technologies, and promoting green practices.

The group arrived at the factory and were greeted by Mr Yang, who led them on a tour of the facility. The group donned protective gear before entering the factory floor, where they were met with the hum of machinery and the clanging of metal. While walking through the factory, Ian was struck by the magnitude of the operation. The vast expanse of the factory and the colossal machinery were a testament to the enormity of the aluminium industry. As the tour progressed, Ian observed the complex production process, with each step being meticulously executed to produce high-quality aluminium products.

Mr Yang explained that the factory produced aluminium products for various industries, including automotive, aerospace, and construction. As they walked through the production lines, Ronny and the other researchers asked questions about the factory's energy usage and carbon emissions. Mr Yang proudly pointed out the state-of-the-art equipment and processes that had been implemented to reduce the factory's environmental impact. He explained that they had invested in energy-efficient technologies, such as regenerative furnaces, which could recover and reuse heat from the melting process. They also had a closed-loop water system that recirculated water to minimize wastewater discharge.

Mr Yang also expressed his concern about the impact of the new regulations on the factory's business and asked Ronny and his team for their suggestions on how to balance environmental protection with economic growth. Ronny and his team offered several suggestions, such as the use of carbon capture technology and more efficient energy consumption. They also discussed the benefits of renewable energy sources, which could help reduce emissions and lower the factory's carbon footprint. Ian was fascinated by the complexity of the challenges facing the factory and the need to balance environmental sustainability with economic growth.

After the productive meeting that lasted the whole afternoon, Ronny, Ian, and Professor Chen decided to conclude their day with an early dinner at a delightful local restaurant, where they could continue their discussions in a more relaxed setting. The group indulged in a variety of mouth-watering dishes, from steamed crab and grilled fish to flavourful vegetables, all while exchanging stories and laughter. Over dinner, they engaged in a thoughtful conversation about the challenges confronting the Hangzhou Bay Industrial Zone and the nation as a whole. They discussed the trade-off between rapid economic growth and environmental degradation, and the new regulations that were being implemented to combat the issue. However, as they stepped outside after finishing their meal, Ian couldn't help but notice the change in the air quality. The once-clear sky was now shrouded in a thick and heavy fog.

'What's going on?' he asked Ronny.

'It's a phenomenon known as "disguised pollution,"' Ronny explained. 'It's when factories release pollutants during off-peak hours when there are fewer people around to monitor their activities. We've been researching ways to address this problem, and it's something we're actively working to combat. The fact that the pollution is visible even at night shows just how serious the problem is and how urgent the need for action is.'

'Ronny, I was wondering, is disguised pollution a problem only in the Hangzhou Bay Industrial Zone or is it a nation-wide issue in China?' asked Ian.

Professor Chen said, 'Actually, Ian, I came across a study recently that suggests disguised pollution is a nation-wide issue in China.'

Ian said, 'Oh, really? That's interesting. How did they come to this conclusion?'

Professor Chen smiled, 'The researchers wanted to see if factories were intentionally polluting more at night when no one could see them. To do this, they looked at pollution levels recorded by 1,583 monitoring stations all over China between 2015–17. Some of these stations were near factories, while others were not. They compared the pollution levels at the stations near factories to the levels at stations not near factories, both before and after sunset. This allowed them to see if there was a difference in pollution levels at night near factories compared to during the day. They found that factories were intentionally polluting more at night, when it was dark, to avoid detection.'

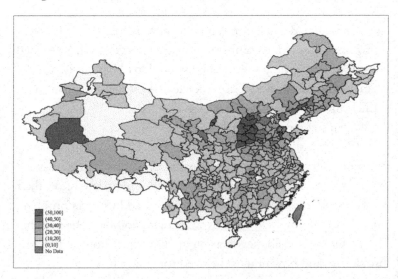

Figure 5.2: Average hourly SO$_2$ in 1,583 monitoring stations from 2015–17

Source: The figure was made using ArcGIS, based on the data downloaded from http://beijingair.sinaapp.com/, sourced from the National Urban Air Quality Live Update Platform at http://106.37.208.233:20035/ (accessed October 20, 2023).

Note: This figure displays the average hourly concentration of SO_2 in 1,583 monitoring stations from 2015–17. The data utilized in this study was obtained from the Ministry of Environmental Protection (MEP), which publishes hourly measurements of PM2.5, PM10, CO, SO_2, NO_2, O_3, and AQI for each station.

Ian sighed, 'I see. So, the study is based on national data, it isn't just specific to the Hangzhou Bay Industrial Zone.'

Professor Chen nodded in agreement, 'Yes, that's correct. The researchers found that the problem of disguised pollution is pervasive across the country and is a significant contributor to China's air pollution crisis.'

This practice has negative impacts on public health and the environment, and the authors call for more effective monitoring and regulation to address it. They suggest potential solutions such as increasing public awareness and using satellite technology to detect nighttime emissions.

Agarwal et al. (2020) found that there is a 10.8 per cent increase in SO_2 emissions in the four hours after sunset near factories in China, compared to the six hours before sunset. This disguised pollution occurs at night when monitoring is less likely to occur. The researchers took into account different factors like atmospheric conditions, electricity generation, winter heating, and traffic to ensure the results were reliable. The research suggests that disguised pollution is not due to atmospheric conditions alone and that firms in key regions are less likely to under-report their emission readings after sunset than firms in non-key regions. The study also found that disguised pollution varies with political factors such as political turnover and central inspection, with pollution being higher after a turnover of the municipal party secretary. Additionally, a decline in GDP growth rate in the previous year increases the magnitude of disguised pollution in the current year.

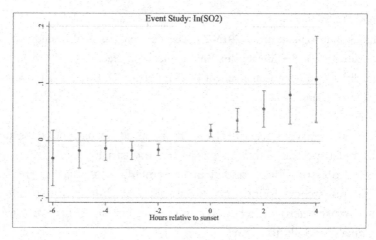

Figure 5.3: Event study (sunset)

Source: Agarwal, S., Han, Y., Qin, Y., and Zhu, H. (2023). 'Disguised pollution: Industrial activities in the dark.' *Journal of Public Economics*, 223.
Note: The figure illustrates the coefficients and corresponding 95 per cent confidence intervals of the event study. The event time is defined as the sunset hour, while the baseline average refers to the first hour before sunset.

'I've been doing some research on the impact of sulphur dioxide emissions from industrial fuels,' Professor Chen said. 'It's pretty concerning. The concentration of SO_2 in off-gases is largely dependent on the sulphur content in different fuels. The industrial sector is the biggest contributor to SO_2 emissions in China.'

Ian nodded, 'That's right. It's a big problem that the government has been trying to tackle. They've been implementing policies to force industrial firms to upgrade their technologies and enhance their fuel standards.'

Ronny replied, 'Yes, but even with the latest technologies, there's still a risk of exceeding regulatory levels. That's why the environmental regulators require polluting firms to install end-of-pipe pollutant scrubbers. It's costly to install and operate, but it's necessary to reduce pollutant concentrations.'

Professor Chen agreed, 'But it's not just the installation and operating costs that are problematic. The sorbent materials used in the scrubbers produce a substantial amount of gypsum or lime sludge that's difficult to dispose of, further adding to the running costs of the scrubbers.'

'To reduce SO_2 emissions, the Chinese government has implemented a number of policies since 2001,' Ronny said. 'And they've been effective, reducing emissions by 28 per cent from 2001–05, and a further 14 per cent from 2006–10.'

'That's impressive,' Ian said. 'What are the recent policies that are influencing firms' behaviour?'

'Well, there are two major measures,' Ian said. 'The first is the implementation of Continuous Emissions Monitoring Systems (CEMS), which collects real-time emission data from above-scale polluters.'

'That sounds like a good idea,' Ian said. 'But are there any limitations to CEMS?'

'The installation and maintenance costs are high, so only large firms have adopted it,' Professor Chen explained. 'And small and medium–sized firms, who often have lower production and pollutant removal technologies, have strong incentives to disguise their polluting behaviour. Plus, even large firms can interfere with the operation of CEMS by various means.'

'So, CEMS may not be as effective as it seems,' Ronny said.

'Right, it depends on local regulatory pressures,' Professor Chen said. 'For example, in key regions facing tough new emission standards, there's a weak association between the SO_2 measurements reported from CEMS and the observations from satellite data. It suggests that the coal power plants may game the system with the MEP on reported data quality when facing high regulatory pressures.'

'That's not good,' Ian said. 'What's the other regulatory measure?'

'The other measure is inspections by local bureaus and the central government,' Ronny said. 'But they have limitations too. With limited resources, local regulators rely on reports of suspicious environmental issues from local residents via social media or official online message boards. And there's often a time lag between observing pollutant discharges and evidence collection.'

'So, how effective are these inspections?' Ian asked.

'Based on anecdotal news and official documents, the local authorities recognize the existence of firms' illegal discharge behaviour,' Professor Chen said. 'They conduct irregular inspections at night to complement other measures such as CEMS monitoring or regular surveillance on industrial sites. And the MEP conducted inspections across all the provinces in China from December 2015 to August 2017, dispatching more than 5,000 inspectors to local sites.'

'But even with thousands of inspectors, they can't cover all the polluting sites, right?' Ian said.

'Exactly,' Professor Chen said. 'Especially if the firm's game the inspectors by disguising their polluting behaviour.'

A recent study published in Proceedings of the National Academy of Sciences (PNAS) entitled 'Quantifying coal power plant responses to tighter SO_2 emissions standards in China' examines how coal power plants in China responded to new emissions standards that were implemented in 2014. The study found that the majority of plants did not reduce their emissions to meet the new standards, but instead chose to pay fines for non-compliance.

The researchers used satellite data to track SO_2 emissions from coal power plants across China and found that there was a significant increase in emissions from non-compliant plants following the implementation of the new standards.

This increase in emissions from non-compliant plants was enough to offset the emissions reductions made by compliant plants, resulting in no net decrease in emissions across the industry as a whole. The study suggests that the fines for non-compliance were not significant enough to incentivize most plants to make the necessary investments in emissions control technology, and that stricter penalties may be needed to encourage greater compliance with environmental regulations. The findings have important implications for efforts to reduce air pollution in China, which has some of the highest levels of pollution in the world.

Ian turned to Ronny. 'Did you remember the crackdown the government did back in 2015? I remember the air was really bad out there and hard to breathe sometimes.'

Ronny nodded. 'Yeah, the authorities implemented rotated inspections across provinces to enforce environmental regulations more strictly. The idea was that it would increase awareness and knowledge among local officials and lead to permanent reductions in pollution.'

Ian asked, 'So, what's the process for these inspections?'

'It's divided into four stages. The first stage is preparing the inspection team, then the second stage is on-site inspection. The third stage is review and feedback, where they evaluate performance and commonly find a lack of leadership experience in the environmental aspect. And the fourth stage is rectification and enforcement, where they submit a plan to the State Council on how they will enforce environmental policies in the future,' Ronny explained.

'Did you hear about the working paper on China's environmental crackdowns?' Professor Chen turned to Ronny. Both Ronny and Ian looked at her curiously.

'It's a really interesting study,' Professor Chen continued. 'The authors analysed the impact of China's environmental crackdowns on polluting firms and found that while there were some short-term improvements, many firms reverted to their previous behaviour after the crackdowns ended.'

According to a recent working paper presented by Karplus and Wu, the earliest time that firms were informed of inspection teams' impending arrival was six weeks in advance, while the majority were only notified a few days prior. Interestingly, SO_2 emissions began to decline slightly when firms received advance warning. During the on-site period, the level of SO_2 emissions was at its lowest within a window of -12 to $+36$ weeks of the inspection team's arrival. However, after the teams left, the SO_2 emission levels returned to their baseline within a timeframe of $+24$ to $+26$ weeks. Although the research suggests that the most polluting plants made the greatest efforts to clean up their act during the crackdown, there was virtually no difference in the distribution of SO_2 pollution following the crackdown.

Ian scratched his head. 'So, what you're saying is that the dirtiest plants cleaned up the pollution the most during the crackdown, but after the crackdown, there was no virtual difference between the SO_2 pollution distribution?'

'Exactly,' Professor Chen confirmed. 'And did you know that environmental awareness varies with income level? Citizens in wealthier cities are more sensitive to plant pollution levels. That's why complained plants show a decreased SO_2 level because they anticipate scrutiny during the inspection phase. But upper-state firms are more likely to receive a complaint when compared with lower-state firms, which is in line with the finding that environmental awareness increases with income.'

Ian nodded thoughtfully; his interest piqued. 'Wow, that's really interesting. What about the methods they found to reduce SO_2 pollution?'

Ronny grinned. 'There are three ways to reduce SO_2 pollution: running pollution control equipment, switching to coal with low sulphur content, and reducing plant output. Scholars found that during the inspection period, low-sulphur coal and SO_2 control equipment—scrubbers—were used to reduce gas emissions. But reducing plant output is only partially causing lower SO_2 emissions.'

Ian was intrigued. 'What about scrubbers? Did they have any effect on SO_2 emissions?'

Professor Chen nodded. '80 per cent of the firms in the scholars' sample had installed scrubbers, but running a scrubber is costly. Moreover, SO_2 is invisible, and the likelihood of detection during the post-period was low.'

Ian thought for a while and said, 'I think the scholars are right about the importance of incentives. Regulators need to have a strong motivation to monitor the pollution level, otherwise, they may not be as effective in implementing the regulations. But it's not just about providing incentives to regulators. We also need to think about how to provide incentives to the firms to improve their environmental performance.'

Ronny added, 'Yes, and we also need to address the issue of collusion in hierarchies that scholars have highlighted. This could be challenging, especially if the central government has limited knowledge and is faced with multiple competing objectives.'

Professor Chen nodded in agreement. 'I agree with both of you. Incentives are crucial, but we also need to focus on improving the environmental quality measurement continuously. Furthermore, involving citizens in the monitoring process could also increase the effectiveness of the crackdowns.'

Ian responded, 'Yes, I think engaging citizens in the monitoring process could be really helpful. This could increase the legitimacy of the crackdowns and help to expand the state's capacity to detect violations.'

Ronny chimed in, 'And if citizens are involved in the process, they could facilitate sustained improvements in the long run, in terms of externalities management and economic priorities.'

Professor Chen smiled, 'I'm glad we're all on the same page. These are important issues that we need to address if we want to see sustained improvements in China's environmental quality.'

'How about in other countries, Ronny? Do you think they face similar challenges?' Ian asked, intrigued by the topic of their discussion.

'Well, based on what I've read recently, it seems that many countries are facing similar challenges when it comes to SO_2 emissions,' he replied.

'Really?' Ian was interested to hear more. 'What have you been reading?'

'I've been reading a recent paper by Zou,' Ronny explained. 'It's about how regulators in the US only monitor emissions intermittently, which can lead to polluting firms taking advantage of the situation and increasing their emissions during unmonitored periods.'

Ian was intrigued. 'Can you tell me more about it?'

'Absolutely,' Ronny replied. 'Basically, the paper reveals that when the government monitors air quality only once every six days under the Clean Air Act, polluting activities tend to change in response.'

'Yes, that's an important study. The authors used thirteen years of satellite observations to construct an indirect measure of particulate pollution. This measure allowed them to observe air quality both during monitors' "on-days" and "off-days,"' Professor Chen explained.

'Interesting. So, what did they find?' Ian asked.

'They found that there was a significant pollution gap between on-days and off-days around monitoring sites that follow the 1-in-6-day schedule. The satellite detected 1.6 per cent less particulate pollution during on-days than during off-days, while pollution levels during off-days do not differ significantly from each other.

The effect size is comparable to the average difference in air quality observed between weekdays and weekends,' Ronny said.

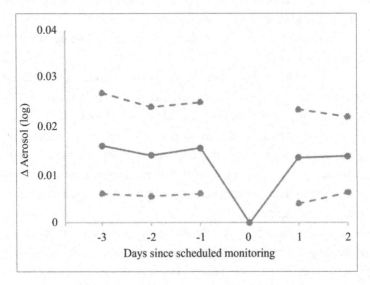

Figure 5.4: The pollution gap: off-days
vs. on-days pollution differences

Source: Zou, E. Y. (2021). 'Unwatched pollution: The effect of intermittent monitoring on air quality.' *American Economic Review*, *111*(7), 2101–26.

Note: The figure displays the pollution concentration trajectory across days of a 1-in-6-day monitoring cycle. The sample comprises all sites with at least one 1-in-6-day PM monitor. Pollution levels are measured using satellite-based aerosol concentration within the 10 km x 10 km area containing the monitoring site. Day 0 corresponds to the scheduled monitoring day, which is normalized to 0. The regression depicted is not conditional on any covariates. Dashed lines represent 95 per cent confidence intervals constructed using standard errors clustered at the county level.

'That's pretty alarming. So, why is there such a big difference in pollution levels between on-days and off-days?' Ian asked.

'The author suggests that gaming occurs during "critical" times when counties' noncompliance risk is high. It's likely that short-term cutbacks of polluting activities occur during these times to avoid detection,' Ronny said.

'That's really interesting. But who is responsible for this gaming?' Ian asked.

'The study paper also suggests that local government coordination may play a role in this strategic behaviour. For example, the author analysed local governments' issuance of public air quality advisories, and found that there was a significant, 10 per cent higher likelihood that an advisory is issued on PM monitoring days. This suggests that there is coordination among local governments to reduce polluting activities on monitoring days,' Ronny explained.

'That's really interesting. It shows that the incentive to avoid monitoring is driving changes in polluting activities, and that a capacity to respond also matters,' Ian said, deep in thought.

'Yes, and areas with large pollution gaps tend to have higher pollution levels, a history of receiving penalties for violations, and the presence of intermittent monitoring sites. Having a high concentration of wood product manufacturers, a highly polluting industry that often operates at partial production capacity, also stands out as a strong predictor of large pollution gaps,' Professor Chen added.

'So, there are some key factors that are driving this strategic behaviour, and local governments are playing a role in coordinating emission reductions. It's really important that we address these issues to ensure clean air for everyone,' Ian said, determinedly.

'Absolutely. It's important to raise awareness about this issue and work together to find solutions,' Ronny agreed.

Ian nodded, feeling a sense of concern and unease. He had always been aware of the environmental challenges in China, but he had never fully grasped the extent of the problem.

The research opened his eyes to the reality of the situation and the urgent need for action.

As they walked back to Ronny's car, they passed by several factories still operating at full capacity, despite the late hour. Ian could see the smokestacks emitting thick clouds of smoke into the air, and he could feel the pollution in his lungs.

'I hope that this research can help address the problem of disguised pollution and contribute to a more sustainable future,' Ronny said.

'I'm sure it will,' Ian replied. 'The work you and your team are doing is so important, and I'm grateful for the opportunity to learn more about it.'

As they drove back to Shanghai, Ian couldn't shake off his concern about the environment. He realized that the challenges facing China were immense and that addressing them would require significant changes in the way we live, work, and consume. But he also felt a sense of hope, knowing that there were people like Ronny and his colleagues who were working tirelessly to make a difference. The visit to the industrial park had opened Ian's eyes to the complexity of the challenges facing China and the urgent need for action. It had also inspired him to think more deeply about his own role in promoting sustainability and protecting the environment.

Chapter 6

Clear Skies, Clear Insights:
The Huai River Heating Policy

After Ian's productive trip to Hangzhou Bay Industrial Zone, he flew to visit his beloved grandparents in the city of Yulin, located in the north of Shaanxi province. Yulin was the place where he'd spent most of his childhood summers, visiting his grandparents who lived in a cozy apartment near the city centre. The city was located to the north of the Qinling–Huai River line, a region famous for its scenic beauty and rich cultural heritage. Ian had fond memories of exploring the nearby Qinling Mountains with his grandfather, who taught him about the different species of flora and fauna that called the mountain range their home.

As the plane began its descent towards Yulin, Ian's attention was drawn to the breathtaking view outside his window. In the distance, he could see the magnificent Qinling Mountains rising up from the earth, their jagged peaks standing tall against the clear blue sky. But as the plane flew closer towards the city, the sky became hazy, and the view became obscured. The severity of the haze increased, shrouding the landscape in a thick, grey mist.

As Ian approached the baggage claim, he spotted his grandparents waiting for him. They both looked incredibly happy to see him, with big smiles on their faces. 'Ian, my dear grandson, it's so good to see you, how was your flight?'

'It was good,' replied Ian. 'The view of the Qinling Mountains from the airplane was amazing. I couldn't stop looking out the window.'

His grandparents both smiled. 'Yes, the Qinling Mountains are one of the most beautiful natural wonders of our country,' said his grandmother. 'We'll have to take you up there for a hike while you're here.'

Ian felt a sense of excitement at the prospect of exploring the mountains again with his grandfather. 'That would be amazing,' he said. 'I remember all the stories you used to tell me about the different plants and animals up there.' Ian's grandfather, a respected geography teacher in the local high school, smiled and added, 'As a geography teacher, I've always emphasized the importance of the Qinling Mountains in our region. They have shaped our landscapes, influenced our climate, and provided a sense of identity for generations. Even today, they stand as a significant natural boundary, dividing the northern and southern regions of our country.'

Ian nodded and replied, 'Yes, I read about that. The Qinling Mountains are also important for the environment, aren't they?'

'Absolutely,' said Ian's grandfather, 'The Qinling Mountains and the Huai River are closely linked. They form a natural boundary between the Yangtze and Yellow River drainage basins, and they both play a critical role in maintaining the ecological balance of our country.'

The Qinling Mountains are an east–west mountain range that, together with the Huai River, separate the Yangtze and Yellow River drainage basins, forming a natural boundary between northern and southern China. Revered as the 'central park of China', the Qinling Mountains are renowned for their rich biodiversity, comprising a diverse range of plants and wildlife. They play a significant role in providing essential environmental functions, including climate regulation, soil conservation, water maintenance, and biodiversity conservation, making them a vital ecological asset of China. Figure 6.1 illustrates the geographical location of this mountain range, which lies between 33.03° and 34.25° latitude.

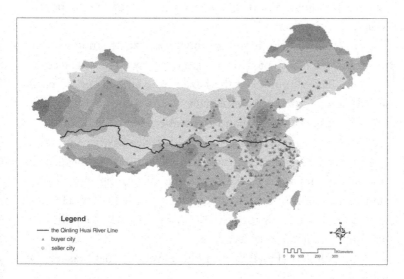

Figure 6.1: China's Qinling–Huai River Line
and PM10 in major cities

Source: Agarwal, S., Wang, L., and Yang, Y. (2023). 'Online Consumption Response to Sustained Exposure to Air Pollution: Evidence from a Quasi-experiment in China.' Working Paper.

Note: This figure shows a map of China with the locations of cities where buyers and sellers are located. The cities where buyers are located are marked with red triangles, while cities where sellers are located are marked with green circles. The black line indicates the Qinling–Huai River Line. The map also includes colours that represent the levels of a particular air pollutant called PM10. The colours range from blue and green for lower levels of PM10 to orange and red for higher levels. These colours are based on data collected from monitoring stations near the buyer cities between January 2017 and September 2019, using a method called ordinary kriging to estimate the levels of PM10 at locations between the monitoring stations.

As they made their way out of the airport, Ian's grandfather started telling him about the changes that had taken place in Yulin since his last visit. 'The city has grown so much,' he said. 'There are new buildings, new restaurants, and new shops. It's almost like a different city now.'

Ian couldn't help but notice the thick haze of smog that hung in the air when they passed through the busy streets of Yulin.

'Ian, have you noticed the haze in the air?' his grandmother asked, noticing the look on his face.

'Yes, it's a lot worse than I remember,' Ian replied.

'There are many reasons for it,' his grandfather chimed in. 'One of them is the increasing traffic pollution from the growing number of cars in the city. Also, the manufacturing activities have significantly contributed to the worsening air quality. However, another important factor is the Qinling–Huai River policy that was implemented a few decades ago.'

'The Qinling–Huai River policy? What's that?' asked Ian, intrigued.

'It is a policy the Chinese government implemented in the 1950s,' his grandfather explained, 'because the winters in the north are much colder than the south, and they wanted to make sure that people had access to heat. The idea was to provide free heating to households north of the Qinling–Huai River Line to help them keep warm during the winter months.'

Ian turned to his grandfather and asked, 'Do you know when heating is provided in Yulin? I've heard that northern cities receive free heating during the winter months, but I read that cities like Xi'an in the south don't have access to heating infrastructure.'

'That's correct,' his grandfather replied. 'Northern Chinese cities received free unlimited heating between November and March. In contrast, heating was largely non-existent in the south because the government did not supply a heating infrastructure, nor was there a private sector to supply it until recently. Indeed, it is widely recognized that winters are cold and uncomfortable in cities that are just south of the Huai River, like Nanjing, Shanghai, and Chengdu.'

'So, providing free heating is a good thing, right?' Ian said.

His grandmother shook her head. 'Not necessarily. The unintended consequence of this policy was that people in the north of the Qinling Mountains use centralized coal-fired system for heating, which releases a lot of pollutants into the air. And the government didn't consider the long-term consequences of their policy.'

'Well, compared to air conditioners, the coal-fired heating system contribute more to the air pollution,' added his grandfather, 'It was supposed to bring heat to the northern part of China during the winter months, but it caused so much pollution instead. The policy created a stark difference in air pollution between north and south of the Qinling Mountains.'

Ian thought about it for a moment. 'But if it's causing pollution, why don't they just use something else for heating?'

'Good point,' his grandma said. 'But it's not that simple. Coal is the cheapest and most widely available source of heating in the north. And it's hard to switch to something else overnight.'

From 1950–80, when China was under central planning, the government provided free coal for fuel boilers to ensure free winter heating in homes and offices as a fundamental right. As a result of budgetary constraints, this right was limited to north China, defined by the line created by the Huai River and Qinling Mountain range. Even today, the northern region continues to use long-standing heating systems, which are heavily reliant on coal and characterized by low efficiency. The use of coal-fired boilers and combined heat and power generators consume more energy compared to more advanced heating systems that rely on electricity, gas, or oil (Wang, et al. 2000). Typically, residential buildings utilize boilers to burn coal and heat water, which is then distributed through iron pipes to each household. However, the long distances that the heated water must travel before reaching individual households contribute to substantial energy loss in the system (Almond, et al. 2009).

However, the incomplete combustion of coal in these boilers leads to the release of at least three measured types of air pollutants, particularly particulate matter that can be highly detrimental to human health (Dockery DW, et al., 1993; Pope CA, 3rd, et al., 2002). Chen et al. (2013) find that to the north of the Qinling Huai River line, ambient concentrations of total suspended particulates are 55 per cent higher, with a mean of 184 μg/m3, and life expectancies were found to be 5.5 years lower, primarily due to an increased incidence of cardiorespiratory illness. The study estimates that the Huai River policy had a significant impact on the lives of 500 million residents in northern China during the 1990s, resulting in a staggering loss of over 2.5 billion life years. According to Ebenstein et al. (2017), the Huai River heating policy caused airborne particulate matter smaller than 10 μm (PM10) concentrations that were 46 per cent higher in the north, reaching 41.7 μg/m3, and resulting in reduced life expectancies of 3.1 years in the north due to higher rates of cardiorespiratory mortality.

Ian expressed his concern to his grandfather, 'Do you know if any other government policies related to public health might have changed at the Qinling–Huai River line? I'm worried that if the government used the river as a boundary for modifying other policies, the impact of pollution on health may not be accurately estimated.'

Grandfather nodded and acknowledged Ian's concern, saying, 'That's a valid point. However, the Huai River is not a border used for administrative purposes. Instead, it was chosen as a dividing line based on the average temperature in January, with the aim of providing free heating to areas north of the river.'

Grandmother chimed in and added, 'The decision to use the Huai River as a dividing line was based on physical geography and climate of the region, rather than political or administrative boundaries. Therefore, it's less likely that changes in other government policies related to public health were correlated with the location of the Huai River.'

After Ian and his grandparents arrived home from the airport, Ian quickly settled in and unpacked his bags. However, he couldn't stop thinking about the Qinling–Huai River policy and its impact on the environment. He had heard about the policy before, but never really delved deep into its effects until now. Driven by curiosity, he eagerly opened his computer and started searching for information. Soon he came across a study that caught his attention.

'Hey, Grandma, Grandpa,' Ian called out, looking up from his computer where he had been researching. His grandparents were sitting beside him, engaged in their own activities. Grandma was knitting a cozy blanket, while Grandpa was flipping through an old photo album.

'Did you know that air pollution is affecting people's decisions to purchase health insurance in China?' Ian continued, sparking their curiosity.

'No, we didn't know that. How is that possible?' Grandpa asked, intrigued. They leaned in closer, eager to hear more. 'I'm reading this paper by Chang, Huang, and Wang,' Ian said, turning his computer screen toward his grandparents. 'They used transaction-level data from a large Chinese insurance company to examine how idiosyncratic variation in daily air pollution affects an individual's decision to purchase or cancel health insurance.'

'That's interesting. I didn't think air pollution would be a factor in health insurance,' Grandma said.

'Me neither. But according to the paper, when air pollution is high, individuals are more likely to purchase insurance contracts.

In addition, insurance contracts are more likely to be cancelled if air pollution improves during the government-mandated 10-day "regret period,"' Ian said, summarizing the paper's findings.

'That's surprising. So, it seems like people are more concerned about their health when the air quality is poor,' Grandpa said.

'Yes. The paper found that a one-standard deviation increase in the daily level of PM2.5 in a city leads to a 7.2 per cent increase in the number of insurance contracts sold in that city that day,' Ian said.

'That's a significant increase,' Grandma said.

'It sure is. The paper also found that pollution affects the aggregate level of insurance contracts sold, rather than changing the timing of insurance purchase,' Ian added.

'That's a lot of information to take in. Did the paper discuss any reasons for these findings?' Grandpa asked.

'Yes, they explored several rational and psychological explanations, with the greatest support found for two mechanisms: projection bias and salience,' Ian explained. 'Projection bias, in particular, is an interesting concept,' he continued, 'as it refers to the tendency for individuals to overestimate how much their future preferences will resemble their current preferences.'

Grandpa looked puzzled. 'What do you mean, Ian? How can someone overestimate their own preferences?'

Ian explained, 'Well, let's say someone really enjoys spicy food. They might assume that they will always enjoy spicy food in the future, even if their tastes change over time. This projection bias can affect the choices people make when it comes to purchasing goods and services.'

Grandma chimed in, 'But how does that impact real-world markets, Ian?'

Ian responded, 'That's a great question, Grandma. The evidence on projection bias in real-world markets is still somewhat limited, but there have been some fascinating studies.

One particularly interesting study was conducted by Conlin and his research team in 2007. They found that weather conditions can actually influence catalogue orders for weather-related clothing items. Specifically, they discovered that lower temperatures on the order date resulted in a higher rate of returns for cold-weather items. It's quite intriguing how our perceptions of the future can be influenced by current circumstances.'

Grandpa looked interested. 'That's really surprising, Ian. So, people are returning items just because the weather was different than what they expected when they made the purchase?'

Ian nodded in agreement. 'Yes, it does appear to be the case. Interestingly, there have been other studies that have discovered similar effects. Take, for instance, a study conducted by Simonsohn in 2010, which revealed that weather conditions can actually impact college enrolment decisions. Additionally, Busse and colleagues conducted a study in 2015 that found weather can influence the choice of automobile people purchase. It's remarkable how external factors like weather can influence our decision-making processes.'

Grandma looked thoughtful as she paused her knitting. 'So, if people are feeling healthy at the moment, they might think they won't need insurance in the future and cancel their policy,' she mused. Her furrowed brow expressed concern as she continued, 'That sounds like a bad idea. What if they get sick and need medical treatment?'

Ian nodded: 'Exactly. That's why projection bias can lead to suboptimal decisions. People might cancel their insurance policies when they don't actually want to, and then regret it later when they need medical care.'

Ian continued, 'Another important concept that might explain the impact of air pollution on the purchase and cancellation of health insurance is salience. It refers to the tendency for certain features to disproportionately affect decision-making.'

'Oh, like how certain news stories or advertisements grab our attention and influence our decisions?' asked Ian's grandma.

'Yes, exactly,' Ian replied. 'In our context, when air pollution is high, the risks of pollution-related diseases are more salient or top of mind. This makes people more likely to see the value of health insurance and purchase it. However, when pollution levels drop, the risks of such diseases become less prominent, and people might cancel their insurance policies.'

Ian's grandpa chimed in, 'So, you're saying that people are more likely to cancel their insurance policies when the risk of getting sick is less salient to them?'

'Yes, that's right,' Ian affirmed. 'Salience can help explain both the increase in demand for health insurance during high air pollution levels and the subsequent increase in the cancellation rate when pollution levels drop.'

'I see,' said Ian's grandma. 'It's fascinating how our perception of risk, and the value of insurance can be influenced by factors like that.'

'Indeed,' Ian agreed. 'Understanding these mechanisms is crucial for policymakers and insurance providers to make informed decisions that protect people's health and financial well-being. It also makes me wonder what other aspects of our lives are affected by air pollution,' Ian said, deep in thought.

As they continued their discussion, the doorbell rang. Grandpa went to answer it and returned with a woman in her thirties. 'Ian, come and meet Ling! You were childhood friends, don't you remember?' Grandpa introduced, 'Now Ling is a professor at Southwest University of Finance and Economics, she teaches . . .' Grandpa paused and turned to Ling.

'Household consumption,' Ling smiled and explained, 'I am interested in studying how different factors affect consumer decision-making.'

'Wow, that's a very important field! Household consumption accounts for around 40 per cent of GDP in China,' Ian replied.

Ling nodded. 'Yes, it's a huge part of the economy.'

Grandma gestured for everyone to join her in the living room. The aroma of freshly brewed tea filled the air as they settled into the comfortable couches, ready to delve deeper into their conversation.

'I was reading an article about it just now. Apparently, some people are concerned about the long-term effects of air pollution on their health, so they're looking into health insurance as a way to protect themselves,' said Ian.

'Wow, that's really interesting!' said Ling. 'In fact, I recently read a study that found a link between air pollution and household consumption. The study found that prolonged exposure to air pollution can cause individuals to change their consumption behaviour, particularly when it comes to purchasing air purifiers.'

Ian's grandparents, nodded in agreement. 'Yes, air pollution is a big problem in China,' said Grandpa. 'I remember when I was young, air pollution was never an issue. But now, it seems like it's everywhere. But I think people are willing to pay more for clean air these days. After all, we see so many air purifiers being sold in stores.'

'That's exactly what this research paper is about,' Ling chimed in. 'It's a research paper written by Ito and Zhang, published in the *Journal of Political Economy*. The authors wanted to find out how much people are willing to pay for clean air, and they did it by studying how people buy air purifiers.'

'Oh, that's fascinating,' said grandfather. 'How did they do it?'

'Well, they looked at sales data for air purifiers in Chinese cities from 2006 to 2014,' Ling explained. 'They also collected data on air pollution levels and city demographics. And to deal with the fact that air pollution and prices might be related, they used a clever trick called a spatial regression discontinuity design. This design allowed them to use natural variations in air pollution levels induced by the Qinling–Huai River policy to estimate people's willingness to pay for clean air.'

A spatial regression discontinuity design is a research method that studies the causal effects of a treatment or intervention by using a natural boundary to compare observations on either side. For example, imagine a city providing financial incentives to businesses within a specific distance of an urban development zone. Researchers can compare businesses just inside and just outside the boundary to estimate the treatment effect. This design helps control factors and understand the impact of the treatment while considering spatial differences and potential confounding factors. It is a valuable approach used in fields like urban planning, public health, and economics.

'I see,' said Grandpa. 'We were just talking about the Huai River policy.'

Ling nodded and explained, 'Yes, this policy caused much higher levels of air pollution in those cities, which allowed the researchers to compare air purifier sales in those cities with sales in cities south of the river. By comparing the sales of air purifiers in cities with high pollution levels to those in cities with lower pollution levels, they could estimate how much people were willing to pay for clean air.'

'That's very interesting,' said Grandma. 'And what did they find?'

'They found that people in China are willing to pay quite a bit for clean air,' Ling said. 'For example, they found that people are willing to pay about ¥320 (around $32.7) per year to remove the amount of pollution caused by the Huai River policy. Actually, the study found that willingness to pay for clean air is not evenly distributed across the population. People with higher incomes are more willing to pay for air purifiers, while those with lower incomes may not be able to afford them. It's another example of how air pollution exacerbates existing social and economic disparities in China.'

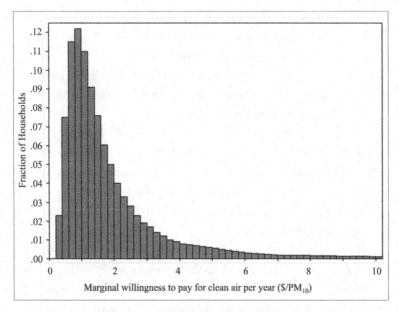

Figure 6.2: Distribution of marginal
willingness to pay for clean air

Source: Ito, K., and Zhang, S. (2020). 'Willingness to pay for clean air: Evidence from air purifier markets in China.' *Journal of Political Economy*, *128*(5), 1627–72.

Note: The histogram presented in this figure is derived from the random-coefficient logit estimation results found in Ito and Zhang (2020). The data used for the histogram is sourced from the household-level annual income data obtained from the 2005 census microdata.

'That's really concerning. It's not fair that some people are more vulnerable to the negative health effects of air pollution just because they can't afford to protect themselves,' said grandfather.

'Well, that just goes to show how important clean air is to people's health and well-being,' said Ian. He turned to Ling, 'How does scientific research measure the effects of air pollution on health?'

Ling smiled. 'Well, there's a new study that just came out that looks at the impact of air pollution on healthcare spending in China,' she said. 'It's quite interesting.'

Ian's grandmother chimed in. 'Isn't it challenging to measure how air pollution affects healthcare spending? There are numerous factors that could influence spending, right?'

'That's true,' Ling said. 'One of the biggest challenges is the potential endogeneity in the pollution exposure data. It could be affected by unobservable factors like economic conditions or avoidance behaviour in response to air pollution.'

Grandmother looked puzzled. 'What do you mean by endogeneity?' she asked.

'Endogeneity means that pollution exposure is related to other factors that can also influence healthcare spending.' Ling explained, 'To accurately understand the impact of pollution, we need to use special techniques like instrumental variables that help us separate the effects of pollution from other factors and get a clearer picture of its true influence.'

Ian nodded thoughtfully. 'It sounds like the researchers put a lot of work into this study,' he said.

Ling nodded in agreement. 'Yes, they did, and the findings are quite remarkable. What's particularly interesting is that the impact of PM2.5 on healthcare expenses varies depending on the type of health facility. For instance, children's hospitals are more than twice as sensitive to PM2.5 levels than other types of facilities.'

Ling added. 'And the study's results are quite robust. They've tested the impact of PM2.5 on healthcare expenses in various ways and found that the effects hold up in both the short and medium terms.'

'So, what does this mean for China?' Ian asked.

'The results show that a permanent reduction of 10 mg/m3 in daily PM2.5 would lead to total annual savings of ¥59.6 billion ($9.2 billion in 2015 terms) in healthcare spending. This amounts to a saving of $22.4 per household per year,' Ling explained. 'Well, if China were to meet the WHO's yearly standard of 10 mg/m3 for PM2.5, it could lead to a reduction of approximately $42 billion in healthcare spending each year,' she continued. 'That's almost 7 per cent of China's total healthcare spending in 2015.'

'That's a significant amount,' Ian said.

'It is, and it's not just the government that pays for it,' Ling replied. 'Individuals also bear the cost of air pollution, whether it's medical bills or purchasing health-related products to cope with the effects of pollution.'

Grandma nodded in agreement. 'Actually, I seem to have purchased more products online during the winter heating season than usual,' she said. 'I wonder if that's related to the air pollution during that time?'

'It could be,' Ling said. 'Studies have shown that people tend to purchase more health-related products online during times of high pollution. I am working on an interesting research project related to online consumption.'

'Really? What is your project about?' asked Grandma.

'We're studying how air pollution affects people's online shopping habits,' explained Ling. 'We want to understand if air pollution has an impact on what people buy online, and if this impact changes over time and continues for a long period. We're also interested in finding out how air pollution affects different types of products and why people may have different shopping behaviours in response to pollution.'

The retail industry has undergone a significant transformation due to the advent of e-commerce, leading to explosive growth in online shopping. This shift has been largely driven by the convenience and cost-effectiveness of online shopping compared to traditional methods. In 2020, the global retail e-commerce market reached a staggering value of $4.28 trillion, with over two billion people purchasing goods and services online (Cramer-Flood, 2021).

China, in particular, has solidified its position as the world's largest e-commerce market, with online retail sales accounting for a substantial 27.2 per cent of the total retail sales in the country in 2022—more than double the figure from 2016 (Ma, 2022). This remarkable growth underscores the increasing significance of e-commerce in China. By 2023, the number of online shoppers in China is projected to reach a staggering 1.14 billion, providing further evidence of the nation's unwavering adoption of e-commerce. Additionally, the COVID-19 pandemic has further fuelled the growth of e-commerce, as more consumers have turned to online shopping to avoid face-to-face contact. Despite this growth, there remains a limited understanding of online consumption compared to offline consumption, due to the lack of detailed, high-frequency data.

'That's quite interesting,' Ian's grandmother looked impressed, and asked. 'But how do you know that air pollution is the cause of the changes in online spending?'

'That's a good question,' said Ling. 'We have used two identification tests to establish the causal relationship between air pollution and online consumption. The first test is a difference-in-differences approach that compares the consumption patterns of cities north and south of the Qinling–Huai River line during the winter heating season. The second test is a two-stage least squares regression discontinuity approach that uses the PM10 concentration along the Qinling–Huai River line as an instrumental variable.'

'Wow, that sounds complicated,' said Grandma. 'But what are the results of your analysis?'

'The results show that air pollution has a significant impact on online consumption. We found that the heating season causes a 7 per cent increase in health-related consumption, a 7.7 per cent increase in consumption of necessities, and a 3.6 per cent decrease in consumption of non-essential goods,' said Ling.

'Wow, that's really interesting,' exclaimed Grandma. 'I had no idea air pollution could have such a significant impact on online consumption habits. I can understand why people would spend more on health-related products when the air quality is bad. But why would people spend less on non-essential goods?'

Ling took a sip of her tea and replied, 'Well, we think that people might be more likely to stay inside when the air quality is bad, and they might not be as interested in shopping for non-essential items.'

Ian nodded in agreement. 'Yes, that makes sense. When the air is bad, I don't feel like going outside at all.'

As they finished discussing the research papers, Ian's grandparents looked at each other with a sense of relief. 'It's great to see the younger generation taking an interest in these issues,' his grandmother said with a smile. 'We've seen firsthand the impact of pollution on our environment and health, and it's heartening to see that people are taking action.'

Ian's grandfather nodded in agreement. 'It's also encouraging to see that researchers are coming up with innovative solutions to combat air pollution,' he said. 'These papers show that there are ways to mitigate the damage and reduce the health costs associated with pollution.'

While enjoying a cup of tea with his grandparents and Ling, Ian felt a genuine gratitude for the meaningful conversation they had shared. As they chatted and exchanged stories, the discussions about sustainable living and healthy choices resonated deeply with him. The importance of these topics sparked a sense of responsibility within Ian, compelling him to spread these values among his peers.

Chapter 7

Smog in the Portfolio:
Air Pollution and Financial Markets

Ian had just arrived in Beijing for a business trip when he received a call from his old friend, Roy. Ian and Roy had met during their university years in the United States and had remained close ever since. Roy was now a fund manager in one of China's largest mutual fund families, and Ian was eager to catch up with him.

'Hey, Ian, how's it going?' Roy greeted him cheerfully over the phone.

'I'm good, Roy, thanks. I just arrived in Beijing this morning. How about you?'

'I'm doing well, thanks. Listen, would you like to come by my office later? I'd love to show you around and catch up.'

Ian was thrilled at the invitation. 'That sounds great, Roy. What's your office address?'

Roy gave him the address, and they arranged to meet later that afternoon. When Ian arrived, he was impressed by the sleek, modern design of the building. Roy greeted him in the lobby and took him up to the thirtieth floor, where his office was located.

'Wow, this is amazing,' Ian said, looking out at the panoramic view of the city.

'I know, right?' Roy replied with a grin as they settled into chairs. 'It's one of the perks of working in finance.'

After catching up for a few minutes, Roy explained that his team was working on an interesting research project investigating the potential impact of air pollution on cognitive bias in financial markets. Ian was intrigued and asked him to explain further.

Roy began by describing how his company had collaborated with researchers from Beijing, Hong Kong, and Singapore to study the relationship between air pollution and cognitive bias. He then handed Ian a copy of a paper titled 'Air pollution, behavioural bias, and the disposition effect in China.'

'This paper is the culmination of months of research and analysis,' Roy explained. 'We wanted to explore whether air pollution, which is a significant issue in many Chinese cities, could exacerbate cognitive biases in financial decision-making.'

Ian skimmed through the paper, scanning the charts and graphs that illustrated the findings. 'This is really interesting,' he said. 'But what do you mean by cognitive bias? And how does air pollution affect it?'

Roy leaned forward in his chair and clasped his hands together. 'Think about it like this,' he said, his eyes bright with excitement. 'Let's say you're deciding whether to invest in a company. You have all the objective data in front of you—financial reports, market trends, and so on. But then, you start to think about how much you like the company's product, or maybe you're influenced by a positive news article you read about them. Suddenly, your decision is no longer solely based on the data, but also on your emotional response to the company.'

Cognitive bias refers to the systematic errors that humans tend to make when processing information and making decisions (Tversky and Kahneman, 1974; Kahneman and Tversky, 1979). These biases can stem from a variety of factors, such as personal beliefs, emotions, or social pressure. In the context of financial markets, cognitive biases can lead investors to make irrational decisions based on incomplete or flawed information, which can ultimately impact their investment outcomes (Barber and Odean, 2000; Thaler, 2015). Understanding and mitigating these biases is a critical part of successful investing, which is why Roy's team's research on the potential impact of air pollution on cognitive bias in financial markets is so important (Li et al., 2021).

Ian nodded along, starting to see the bigger picture. 'And how does air pollution fit into all of this?' he asked.

Roy's eyes sparkled with excitement. 'Well, it's been observed that air pollution can affect cognitive function, specifically in terms of memory and decision-making abilities,' he said. 'So, if we can prove that air pollution has an impact on cognitive bias, it could have significant implications for the financial markets, especially in countries like China where air pollution is a major problem.'

Ian was intrigued. 'And what have you found so far?'

Roy leaned back in his chair, a thoughtful expression on his face. 'Well, it's still early days, but the initial findings are quite compelling,' he said. 'We're seeing a definite correlation between air pollution levels and the disposition effect, which is another behavioural bias that we investigated in our study. It refers to the tendency for investors to hold onto losing investments for too long while selling winning investments too quickly.'

Losing investments refers to those that have declined in value or failed to meet expected returns. These investments may have faced obstacles or setbacks, resulting in a decrease in market value over time. Investors tend to hold on to losing investments longer than they should, driven by psychological biases. Emotions such as fear, hope, or regret play a role in this behaviour as investors believe that these underperforming investments will eventually recover. However, this persistence with unfavourable investments can cause missed opportunities to invest in more promising ventures.

Conversely, winning investments are those that have generated profits or experienced significant value appreciation, exceeding initial expectations and providing substantial returns. Investors often sell their winning investments too quickly in an attempt to secure profits and avoid potential losses. The desire to capitalize on the gains achieved so far may cause investors to overlook potential future growth prospects associated with these successful investments.

The disposition effect can result in a suboptimal portfolio performance. Numerous studies have explored the disposition effect and its impact on financial markets. For example, Barber and Odean (2000) found that individual investors in the United States tend to sell their winning stocks at a much higher rate than their losing stocks. Similarly, research conducted by Xu and Harvey (2015) in China showed that the disposition effect was present in both individual and institutional investors. Another study by Baker and Wurgler (2006) found evidence of the disposition effect in twenty-six international stock markets, including China. These findings suggest that the disposition effect is a global phenomenon that affects investor decision-making regardless of nationality or culture. Additionally, other studies have found that the disposition effect can be affected by various factors, such as investor experience (Dhar and Zhu, 2006) and market conditions (Kumar and Lee, 2006). Overall, understanding the disposition effect is crucial for investors to make better decisions and improve their investment performance.

Ian raised an eyebrow in surprise. 'I had no idea that air pollution could have that kind of effect,' he said.

Roy nodded. 'It's a relatively new area of research, but it's becoming increasingly important as air pollution levels continue to rise in many parts of the world. We need to understand how it affects all aspects of our lives, including financial decision making.'

Ian leaned back in his chair, deep in thought. 'This really puts things into perspective,' he said. 'I mean, we already know that air pollution is harmful to our health, but if it's also affecting our ability to make rational decisions, that's a whole other level of impact.'

Roy grinned and replied, 'Exactly, that's why we're so excited to be collaborating with the researchers on this project. We want to make sure that we're taking all factors into account when making investment decisions. Let me tell you, Ian, this dataset is a gem,' Roy continued, his voice brimming with excitement. 'It's not just comprehensive, covering 773,198 valid investment accounts across seven equity funds from 2007 to 2015, but it also contains complete account-level information for all investors in the company. The investors come from all 31 provinces and 247 cities in mainland China. Our company is one of China's largest mutual fund families.'

Ian leaned forward in his chair, intrigued. 'That does sound impressive. But what makes it particularly useful for your study?'

'It's ideal for examining the effects of air pollution for two reasons,' Roy replied confidently. 'First, as you know, air pollution is one of the most pressing environmental problems facing developing countries, like China and India. So, a proper assessment of this issue could have both academic value and important normative implications. And second, the dataset covers most of China's major cities. This extensive coverage is crucial to our ability to design tests that can accurately identify the influence of air pollution.'

Ian nodded, impressed. 'I see what you mean. With that level of granularity, you should be able to pinpoint the impact of air pollution on investment behaviour much more precisely than previous studies.'

Roy continued his explanation to Ian, 'So to better understand the relationship between the disposition effect and air pollution, we aggregated investor accounts at the same level, and then identified for each investor whether a position in a fund implied a capital gain or a capital loss based on their entire trading history.'

Ian nodded, following along with Roy's explanation. 'I see. And how did you use this data to test the influence of air pollution on the disposition effect?' He asked.

Roy took a deep breath before explaining further. 'Let me give you an example. We started with two cities, A and B, where investors traded the same financial asset. Both cities were exposed to similar levels of air pollution early in the week, but on Wednesday, a strong wind blew away the air pollution in City A, while City B remained the same.

'The team looked at the trading behaviour of investors located in these two cities before and after the drastic drop of Air Quality Index (AQI) in City A. If pollution has a short-term influence, the disposition effect of the treatment group (City A's investors) should decrease in the post-wind period compared with that of the control group (City B's investors) and the treatment-group bias in the pre-wind period.'

Table 7.1: US EPA guide to AQI

Air Quality Index (AQI) Level of Concern	Air Quality Index (AQI)	PM 2.5 Health Effects Statement	PM 2.5 Health Cautionary Statement
Good	0–50	PM 2.5 air pollution poses little or no risk	None
Moderate	51–100	Unusually sensitive individuals may experience respiratory symptoms	Unusually sensitive people should consider reducing prolonged or heavy exertion

Unhealthy for Sensitive Groups	101–150	Increasing likelihood respiratory symptoms in sensitive individuals, aggravation of heart or lung disease and premature mortality in persons with cardiopulmonary disease and the elderly	People with heart or lung disease, older adults, and children should reduce prolonged or heavy exertion
Unhealthy	151–200	Increased aggravation of heart or lung disease and premature mortality in persons with cardiopulmonary disease and the elderly, increased respiratory effects in general population	People with heart or lung disease, older adults, and children should avoid prolonged or heavy exertion; everyone else should reduce prolonged or heavy exertion

Very Unhealthy	201–300	Significant aggravation of heart or lung disease and premature mortality in persons with cardiopulmonary disease and the elderly; significant increase in respiratory effects in general population	People with heart or lung disease, older adults, and children should avoid all physical activity outdoors; everyone else should avoid prolonged or heavy exertion
Hazardous	301 or higher	Serious aggravation of heart or lung disease and premature mortality in persons with cardiopulmonary disease and the elderly; serious risk of respiratory effects in general population	Everyone should avoid all physical activity outdoors; people with heart or lungs disease, older adults, and children should remain indoors and keep activity levels low

Source: Chang, T. Y., Huang, W., and Wang, Y. (2018). Something in the Air: Pollution and the Demand for Health Insurance. *The Review of Economic Studies*, 85(3 (304)), 1609–1634. https://www.jstor.org/stable/26543944 (accessed October 20, 2023).

Ian nodded, starting to understand. 'So, you investigated two versions of the difference-in-differences (DID) test to capture the effect of a drastic dissipation of air pollution in general and that caused by strong winds in particular. How did you conduct these tests?'

'In the first version, the research team identified all city-level observations with high AQIs in the early part of the week and sharp AQI drops of more than two standard deviations, and then created a control group similar to that of City B. We verified that the disposition effect did not differ between the two cities in the pre-wind part of the week and then conducted the DID test. The study found that the disposition effect was significantly attenuated for the treatment group after the drastic reduction in AQI,' Roy explained.

'And in the second version?' Ian prompted.

'In the second version, the researchers identified the treatment group as cities that had high AQIs on Monday/Tuesday and experienced strong winds on Wednesday/Thursday. They conducted a placebo test where both treatment and control cities had no air pollution at the beginning of the week. In this case, a strong wind blowing mid-week did not affect the disposition effect, suggesting that it is changes in AQI introduced by the strong wind that caused the disposition effect observed in our sample,' Roy replied.

Ian nodded, appreciating the thoroughness of the testing. 'It sounds like you've conducted a comprehensive study. Were there any unexpected findings?'

Roy shook his head, a confident smile on his face. 'No, our results remained highly robust even when we employed strong winds as an instrumental variable or utilized different thresholds to define significant AQI decreases alongside strong winds.'

Ian leaned back in his chair; his curiosity piqued. 'That's impressive. So, based on your research, what fascinating correlations have you discovered between air pollution and the disposition effect?'

Roy's eyes lit up with excitement. 'Well, let me share an intriguing insight. We found that cities with high levels of air pollution have a three to four times higher probability of their investors exhibiting a high disposition effect compared to those with medium or low-disposition effects.'

Ian leaned forward, his interest growing. 'That's quite a significant finding. So, what's the next step? How do we establish whether this correlation implies a causal impact of air pollution on trading behaviour?'

Roy paused, considering Ian's question. 'Validating a causal relationship would indeed be compelling. We plan to conduct further research using innovative methodologies, such as natural experiments or quasi-experimental designs, to explore the causal mechanisms underlying the observed correlation.'

Ian spoke eagerly, 'Roy, have you heard of the Huai River policy? It's fascinating. The government created this policy, which unintentionally worsened the air quality of cities north of the river by providing free winter heating to homes and offices only in the urban regions north of the Huai River. The winter heating operates via the provision and burning of free coal for boilers, which release air pollutants.'

Roy nodded, 'Yes, I'm familiar with it. We actually used it in our study. The Huai River policy created a "discontinuity" in terms of AQI along the river, which researchers have used to identify the plausible causal influence of air pollution on life expectancy.'

Ian settled into his chair. 'Tell me more. How did you use it in your study?'

Roy leaned in closer and explained, 'We exploited a quasi-experiment in which government policies generate exogenous variations in air pollution in the geographical cross-section.

Cities located to the north of the Huai River exhibit a significantly higher disposition effect, which we tested using a two-stage specification. We treated the location to the north of the river as an instrument of AQI in the first stage and when we regressed the disposition effect on instrumented AQI in the second stage, we found a significantly positive relation. Moreover, this relationship is highly significant only in the heating seasons, when additional air pollution is created by the free heating policy in northern China.'

Ian's eyes widened, 'That's excellent work, Roy. I'm impressed by the methodology you used to test the effects of air pollution on the disposition effect.'

Another study, 'Pollution and Performance: Do Investors Make Worse Trades on Hazy Days?' (Huang et al., 2020) also examines the impact of air pollution on stock-trading behaviour and performance. The authors hypothesize that air pollution, which decreases cognitive functioning, leads to behavioural biases and a reliance on heuristics in decision-making, negatively affecting trading performance. Using unique account-level equity-transaction data from a large Chinese brokerage house, the study covers 87,054 households from thirty-four cities in China during the period from January 2007 through December 2014. They collected data on over four million investor-dates from a large Chinese brokerage house and matched this data with information on air quality. By doing this, they were able to control for many potential sources of bias that could affect their findings. Specifically, they were able to include information on each investor's trading behaviour over time, as well as the specific dates when trades were made. This allowed them to measure the impact of air pollution on trading performance more accurately.

The study found that air pollution has a negative impact on the stock trading performance of households, even after considering the time of year, weather conditions, and the specific investor. The authors discovered that the worse the air pollution, the more negative the effect on trading performance. For example, when compared to days with good air quality, the trading performance of an investor is 8.26 basis points lower on days with lightly polluted air, 15.35 basis points lower on days with moderately polluted air, 26.81 basis points lower on days with heavily polluted air, and 59.57 basis points lower on days with severely polluted air, assuming a 40-day holding period. This loss is significant and accounts for about 6.80 per cent of the average underperformance of individual investors in the study. Overall, the total loss due to trading on hazy days in China is estimated to be about ¥17.314 billion per year.

To make sure their findings are accurate, the authors of the study conducted additional tests. First, they wanted to make sure that cities weren't manipulating their reported air pollution levels, so they used a density test of McCrary (2008) to identify such cities. More specifically, cities with AQI values exhibiting significant discontinuities around 100—that is, the cut-off for 'blue-sky' days—are classified as manipulator cities. The results continue to hold and become stronger when they exclude trades by investors in manipulator cities. Second, the effect of air pollution on trade performance may become more pronounced when there has been an extended period of air pollution. The authors thus include an indicator for persistent pollution and its interaction terms with air-pollution variables as additional regressors in the baseline regression, finding evidence suggesting that persistent pollution is particularly detrimental to trade performance. Third, to address the concern that trades in local firms may affect the results, the authors conduct a sensitivity analysis by excluding all trades in firms located in the same city as the investor. The results remain robust, indicating that the effect of air pollution is not driven by trading in local firms.

The implications of the study are significant, indicating that air pollution has a substantial impact on individual investor's trading performance, causing significant financial losses. As such, policymakers and investors should take into account the potential effects of air pollution on trading performance when making investment decisions. Furthermore, the study highlights the importance of considering environmental factors in economic decision-making, particularly in emerging markets such as China, where air pollution is a severe problem.

Ian was curious about whether their findings were unique to Chinese investors, or if they had been observed in other countries as well. 'Roy, do you know if anyone else has done research on this topic outside of China?' Ian asked.

Roy proceeded to tell Ian about a paper he had recently read. 'US researchers have also conducted similar studies using data from the New York Stock Exchange (NYSE),' replied Roy. He pulled out his laptop and began to explain. 'Basically, the study looked at the effect of short-term changes in PM2.5 in Manhattan over a fifteen-year period on the daily returns of the S&P 500. They controlled for a wide range of potentially confounding factors, like other air pollutants and meteorological considerations, to isolate the effect of PM2.5 on the stock market.'

Ian listened attentively. 'So, what did they find?'

'They found that a one standard deviation increase in daily ambient PM2.5 concentrations caused a statistically significant 11.9 per cent reduction in daily percentage returns of the S&P 500,' explained Roy. 'The magnitude of this effect is comparable to estimates of the effect of variations in daily weather conditions on returns. The result was remarkably robust to a variety of different assumptions about confounding and a variety of falsification checks.'

Ian looked impressed. 'That's a significant finding. It's similar to what we found in our study of Chinese investors.

Did they investigate the potential mechanisms behind the effect of pollution on the stock market?'

Roy nodded. 'Yes, they did. They examined the effects of PM2.5 on movements in the volatility index (VIX), which measures expected stock market volatility and is widely considered a measure of fear amongst traders. They found that increases in PM2.5 led to increases in the VIX. Furthermore, they decomposed the VIX into its risk and uncertainty elements and found that the effects only existed for the "pure" risk aversion component. These findings suggest that pollution-induced changes in risk appetite may be an important part of the story.'

Recent studies suggest that exposure to PM2.5 may have cognitive effects (Cacciottolo et al., 2017; Power et al., 2018; Zhang et al., 2019). These effects may occur indirectly through impaired respiratory functioning or directly through changes in blood flow and circulation (Gan et al., 2019; Xu et al., 2020). PM2.5 exposure can lead to reduced blood flow to the brain, which can impact cognitive output (Xu et al., 2020). Additionally, PM2.5's small size allows it to enter the brain directly through the olfactory axon, leading to potential neuroinflammation and oxidative stress (Cacciottolo et al., 2017; Zhang et al., 2019). These pollution-induced changes in health can impact decision-making in various ways, including changes in resource allocation and mood.

For local pollution levels to affect same-day stock market returns, there must be a link between pollution and decision-making that is relevant to the market. The researchers proposed several mechanisms that could underpin such a link, including changes in risk appetite, choice bracketing behaviour, and mood. Changes in decisions by marginal investors or market-makers physically located in New York can affect movements in prices on the NYSE. An increase in risk aversion, for example, could lead investors to shift away from risky assets such as stocks, lowering market returns.

Ian expressed fascination and asked Roy about the significance of the study. Roy replied by outlining two key reasons. First, this study presents a novel perspective on pollution's impact on productivity by extending its examination beyond low-skilled outdoor workers. Instead, it sheds light on highly skilled indoor workers in the financial market, revealing a more significant negative influence on workplace performance than previously understood. Second, pollution's effect on stock returns challenges the efficient markets hypothesis, which is a crucial underpinning of market-based economies. In essence, variations in air quality in Manhattan lead to inefficient price signals throughout the broader economy.

'You know, Ian,' Roy said, taking a sip of his coffee. 'I was reading a recent study that suggests air pollution affects not just investors, but also financial analysts.'

Ian raised his eyebrows. 'Really? I hadn't heard about that. What study is this?'

'It's called "Air Pollution, Affect, and Forecasting Bias: Evidence from Chinese Financial Analysts." It was conducted by Dong, Fisman, Wang, and Xu in 2021 and published in the *Journal of Financial Economics*,' Roy replied.

'Interesting. So, what did they find?' Ian asked, leaning forward in his chair.

Roy took a deep breath and began to explain. 'Well, they studied the link between air pollution and financial analyst's earnings forecasts in China. The Shenzhen Stock Exchange has required that all site visits be disclosed since 2009, so the researchers were able to observe the timing of analyst's visits. They identified 3,824 earnings forecasts made by 726 investment analysts in the weeks following corporate site visits during 2009–15.'

Ian nodded, impressed. 'That's a lot of data to work with. And what did they find?'

'Pollution is severe and highly variable across geographies and time in China, providing variation in ambient circumstances that is of such magnitude as to plausibly have a causal impact on analyst affect,' Roy explained 'They found that a city's air quality index on the date of a site visit is negatively correlated with the visiting analyst's subsequent earnings forecast, relative to realized earnings. Essentially, higher air pollution was associated with lower earnings forecasts.'

'That's fascinating. And what about the long-term forecasts?' Ian asked.

'Well, the negative pollution-forecast relation is driven by longer-term forecasts, which involve more guesswork and speculation by the analyst. They also found that the link between pollution and forecast bias dissipates with the time elapsed between visit and forecast, as would be expected if the link between pollution and forecast pessimism were driven by analyst mood during a visit,' Roy replied.

Ian looked thoughtful. 'So, it seems like air pollution can impact not only investors' behaviour but also financial analyst's forecasts. Did they find anything else?'

'They did. They found that the correlation between pollution and pessimism is stronger for firms that do not themselves produce high emissions. This finding helps to rule out the possibility that a firm's own pollution causes a negative inference about its environmental risks or productivity. Additionally, they found that the pessimism associated with pollution disappears for cases in which analysts from different brokerage firms visit the same site on the same date, possibly suggesting a debiasing effect of multiple perspectives,' Roy said.

Ian nodded, taking it all in. 'That's a lot of interesting findings. I wonder if this holds true in other countries as well.'

'It's possible. But the severity and variability of pollution in China make it a natural setting to study this link,' Roy said.

As Ian and Roy continued their discussion, they delved deeper into the ways in which air pollution affects not just the health of individuals, but also the economy as a whole, particularly from the perspective of individual investors and financial analysts. Ian pointed out that the economic impacts of air pollution are often overlooked by investors, but they can be significant. For example, companies operating in polluted areas may face reputational risks and legal liabilities that can affect their financial performance.

Roy agreed and added that air pollution also has a significant impact on behavioural finance, which is the study of how psychological biases affect financial decisions. He explained that people's perception of pollution can influence their investment decisions, leading them to avoid companies that operate in polluted areas or invest in companies that are working to reduce pollution. Roy emphasized that understanding these behavioural biases is crucial for investors to make informed decisions that align with their values and goals.

The two agreed that continued research in this field is crucial to fully understand the scope of pollution's impact on society and the economy, particularly from the perspective of individual investors and financial analysts. Ian mentioned that he had heard of some innovative solutions, such as using green infrastructure and clean energy sources to combat pollution, which can provide investment opportunities that align with environmental responsibility. Roy added that investors could also play a role in driving change by engaging with companies on environmental issues and supporting initiatives that promote sustainability.

As their conversation came to a close, Ian left Roy's office feeling grateful for the opportunity to learn from someone with such deep expertise in the field of behavioural finance. He realized that air pollution's impact on society and the economy is more far-reaching than he had previously thought, and he felt motivated to continue researching this important topic. As he walked out into the bustling streets of Beijing, Ian felt hopeful that with continued efforts from researchers, policymakers, and investors like Roy, society could make progress in mitigating the harmful effects of air pollution and creating a healthier, more sustainable world for future generations.

Chapter 8

Location, Location, Pollution: How Air Quality Impacts Real Estate Markets

Ian sat at the kitchen table, sipping his coffee and flipping through the morning news on his iPad. He came across a headline that caught his attention: 'Hazardous materials truck carrying nitric acid overturns on Arizona highway, prompting evacuations.'

'Wow, this is terrible,' Ian said, turning to his wife Sarah who was making breakfast. 'Apparently a truck carrying nitric acid crashed in Arizona, and people had to be evacuated.'

'Oh my god, that's scary,' Sarah replied. 'I hope everyone is okay.'

Ian continued reading the article, his voice filled with concern. 'It says here that the chemical can cause severe skin burns and eye damage, and it's fatal if inhaled. People within a half-mile radius of the incident were evacuated, and those within one mile of the incident were directed to shelter in place. And it's not just the immediate danger—residents in the area are concerned about the lingering effects of the chemicals in the air, water, and soil.'

Sarah frowned, 'That's a real concern. It's disheartening to hear about the devastating impact on the surrounding ecosystem, with many plants and animals perishing as a result of the accident.'

Ian nodded, 'I can't help but wonder about the potential long-lasting consequences on property values in the area.'

'Speaking of which, have you looked into the air quality in China? We're planning on selling our condo here soon.' Sarah asked.

Ian scratched his chin. 'I haven't yet, but it's definitely something we need to consider. Air pollution is a big problem in China, and it can affect property values,' Ian remarked. 'It's crazy how much air pollution can affect people's health and quality of life.'

Sarah nodded in agreement. 'That's right. We need to keep a close eye on the air quality index and choose the right time to sell the condo, so we can get the best value for it. Nobody wants to buy a property in an area with poor air quality.'

Ian continued, 'But have you heard about the study that came out recently? Apparently, sellers can actually get higher prices for their properties on polluted days.'

Sarah turned around, her eyebrow raised in surprise, and looked at Ian before resuming her cooking. 'Really?' she exclaimed. 'That sounds counterintuitive.'

Ian nodded in agreement. 'Yeah, I was sceptical too, but there was actually a study conducted in China. It found that buyers are willing to pay higher prices for housing on days with increased air pollution. This can be attributed to their tendency for relative thinking or salience.'

Panel A. Local Buyers

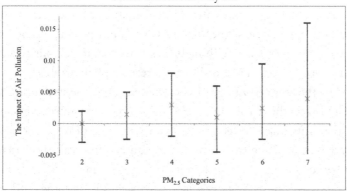

Panel B. Non-local Buyers

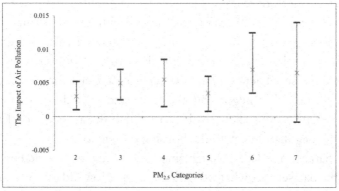

Figure 8.1: The impact of air pollution on unit price

Source: Qin, Y., Wu, J., and Yan, J. (2019). 'Negotiating housing deal on a polluted day: Consequences and possible explanations.' *Journal of Environmental Economics and Management*, 94, 161–87.

Note: These figures plot the impact of air pollution on unit price for local and non-local buyers. Regression coefficients with 95 per cent confidence interval are reported in the graph.

Sarah still looked surprised as she set down her breakfast on the table and joined Ian. 'That's interesting,' she said with a chuckle. 'So, you're suggesting that we could potentially benefit from waiting for a day with higher air pollution to sell our condo? I'm curious to learn more about the research behind this.'

'In this study, Qin and his team examined the impact of air pollution on the real estate market in Beijing. They were interested in the immediate effects of severe air pollution on housing purchases, as these transactions have an economically important outcome,' Ian explained. 'The monetary amount associated with each transaction is large relative to households' income, and the consequences of housing purchases can endure for a long period or even one's entire life.'

Ian continued, 'What's interesting about this study is that Qin's team had access to a major housing brokerage firm's transaction data in Beijing, which had more than 100,000 transactions of resale houses. They were able to record the exact date when the buyer and seller negotiated the price and signed the contract immediately after, allowing them to match the air pollution level of the negotiation day to the housing transactions.'

Sarah nodded, recognizing the unique characteristics of the dataset. 'So, what were the findings? How did they examine the impact of air pollution on housing deal negotiations?' she asked.

Ian went on to explain that Qin's team found that the transaction prices on severely polluted days were 0.65 per cent higher than those of days without pollution, after controlling for various factors. 'Using the average transaction price and volume on a typical day, the calculated total increase in overall value of housing sold is about ¥3.51 million,' Ian said.

'That's quite a significant effect,' Sarah remarked. 'But why would buyers be willing to pay more for a house on a polluted day?'

Ian smiled. 'That's the interesting part. Qin's team suggests that the positive association between air pollution and housing transaction prices is likely due to relative or salience thinking of home buyers. Buyers are willing to pay more for housing on days with higher air pollution due to their perception of a greater improvement in living quality. The negative impact of air pollution on current and potential living conditions makes the increase in living quality more appealing, leading to a higher willingness to pay. This preference for improved living conditions outweighs the focus on price during negotiations.'

Relative thinking is a theory that explains how people make decisions by comparing their choices to other options, rather than judging them independently. This idea is supported by research using lab experiments and real-world data, which has been extensively explored by Azar (2007) and Bushong et al. (2015). Salience theory is a related concept that builds upon relative thinking. It suggests that decision-makers tend to focus more on specific qualities that stand out when considering different options, giving them a greater importance in the decision-making process. This theory is further backed by empirical evidence from studies conducted by Dessaint and Matray (2017) and Hastings and Shapiro (2013).

Sarah nodded, impressed. 'That's a fascinating finding. I have never thought about how air pollution might affect the housing market in Beijing. It's amazing how much we can learn from big data nowadays. But there could be some possible explanations to the findings.'

'What do you mean?' Ian asked.

'It's possible that buyers who sign a contract on polluted days may place a higher value on home ownership in Beijing because going outside on a polluted day would increase their exposure to pollution,' Sarah explained. 'In other words, their sample could be selected.'

'That makes sense,' Ian said. 'But wouldn't the total transaction volume decline if only buyers with a higher valuation of home ownership in Beijing were selected for the sample?'

'Yes, that's a good point,' Sarah replied. 'Did they test that?'

'Yes, the research team tested this hypothesis and found that the transaction volume did not decline, which rules out the possibility that transacted units are different on polluted days.' Ian explained.

Sarah asked, 'Ian, I was wondering if air pollution affects people's cognitive abilities and if that in turn affects the negotiation process and the transaction price?'

Ian responded, 'That's a fascinating question, Sarah. It's a plausible explanation for the effects of air pollution. The authors used heterogeneity analysis to test the hypothesis, identifying local and non-local buyers and estimating the effect separately. If the hypothesis held, the results would be similar for both groups. Contradicting the hypothesis, they found that air pollution significantly increased the transaction price for non-local buyers but had no impact on local buyers, refuting the hypothesis.'

Sarah considered this and asked, 'But couldn't the results be influenced by locals and non-locals having different durations of exposure to air pollution?'

Ian agreed, 'That's a valid concern, but they don't have enough data to test this alternative hypothesis. However, it is reasonable to assume that both locals and non-locals in the sample have been exposed to air pollution for a similar amount of time.'

Sarah nodded and added, 'That makes sense since individuals must have a Beijing hukou or five consecutive years of work experience in Beijing to purchase a unit in the city. Most non-locals with a Beijing hukou are university graduates, indicating they have likely been exposed to air pollution for a significant period of time as well.

'I think this paper's findings are quite significant, Ian. It highlights the vulnerability of buyers to contextual factors like air pollution, and policies could be implemented to reduce the influence of such biases on the housing market transaction process. Do you think that's feasible?'

'I definitely think it's worth exploring, Sarah. One possible solution is to extend the time between the negotiation day and the final contract signing day. This would give buyers more time to think rationally and reduce the magnitude of such biases,' Ian replied.

'That's a great idea, Ian. But what about the housing agents? Could they also be affected by such biases?' Sarah asked.

'Actually, yes. Housing agents could rush buyers and sellers to close the deal on the polluted negotiation day to get more brokerage fees, breaking the market equilibrium and causing more incurred regrets,' Ian explained.

Sarah nodded in agreement and added, 'So, it seems like the impact of air pollution on the housing market is not limited to just buyers and sellers, but also extends to the housing agents involved in the transaction process.'

'The implications of these findings go beyond just the housing market,' Ian continued. 'They also have implications for environmental policy evaluation. We need to raise public awareness of the behavioural consequences of air pollution. Individuals need to be provided with specific information about air pollution levels every day, so they can avoid being exposed to severe air pollution on a severely polluted day.'

Sarah agreed, 'Yes, that's crucial. People need to be educated about how air pollution affects their cognitive abilities, so they can be aware of their biased behavioural consequences due to air pollution.'

'I just read an interesting article on the economic benefits of clean air, Sarah,' Ian said, as he searched through his iPad for the article. 'It turns out that China isn't the only country where researchers have studied the effects of pollution on the housing market. In the US, there have also been studies on this topic.'

Sarah nodded, 'That sounds interesting. But I thought China's air pollution situation was unique.'

Ian continued, 'There's this work by Chay and Greenstone called "Does Air Quality Matter? Evidence from the Housing Market." They use the hedonic approach to estimate the economic benefits of air quality, specifically in relation to federal air pollution regulations in the United States.'

Ian paused as he found the article on his iPad and showed it to Sarah. 'See, there's no explicit market for clean air, so the economic value of this non-market amenity must be estimated using other methods. This study utilizes the framework of the Clean Air Act Amendments to offer fresh insights into how air quality is integrated into housing prices.'

The Clean Air Act Amendments (CAAAs) of 1970, passed by the United States Congress, represent a major shift in air pollution regulation in the country. Prior to this legislation, state governments were primarily responsible for regulating air pollution, and there were few incentives for them to impose strict regulations on polluters. The CAAAs established federal air quality standards, known as the National Ambient Air Quality Standards, for five major pollutants, including total suspended particulates (TSPs). The goal of the amendments was to bring all counties into compliance with the standards by reducing local air pollution concentrations.

To achieve this goal, EPA was tasked with assigning each county to either non-attainment or attainment status for each of the pollutants based on whether the relevant standard was exceeded. States were directed to develop and enforce local air pollution abatement programmes to ensure that each of their counties attained the standards. For non-attainment counties, plant-specific regulations for every major source of pollution were required. These regulations mandated that substantial investments in new or existing plants be accompanied by state-of-the-art pollution abatement equipment and strict emissions ceilings. The 1977 amendments further required that any increase in emissions from new investment be offset by a reduction in emissions from another source within the same county.

States were also required to set emissions limits on existing plants in non-attainment counties. In attainment counties, regulations on polluters were less stringent, with larger-scale investments requiring less expensive pollution abatement equipment and no offsets necessary. Smaller and existing plants were essentially unregulated. To ensure compliance, both the states and the federal EPA were given substantial enforcement powers, with the EPA approving all state regulation programmes to limit variance in regulatory intensity across states, and states running their own inspection programmes and imposing fines for noncompliance. The 1977 amendments made the rules for controlling pollution at specific plants both federal and state law. This gives the EPA the authority to punish states that do not strictly enforce these rules and to penalize plants that violate them. It has been discovered that levels of TSPs and SO_2 decreased significantly more in counties designated as nonattainment than in those designated as attainment during the 1970s (Chay and Greenstone, 2003a; Greenstone, 2004).

Sarah was sipping coffee and turned to Ian, 'So what did this study actually find?'

Ian put down his coffee and began to explain, 'Well, the paper talks about how they used a term called "non-attainment status" as an instrumental variable. This variable helped them to estimate the impact of changes in total suspended particulates (TSPs) concentration on housing prices. The elasticity of housing values with respect to TSPs concentrations ranges from 0.20 to 0.35.'

Sarah looked puzzled and asked, 'What does that mean?'

'This means that a decrease of 10 mg/m3 in TSPs concentration in nonattainment counties, equivalent to a 12 per cent reduction, was associated with an increase in housing prices of approximately 2.5–3.5 per cent,' explained Ian. 'This suggests that clean air is highly valued by individuals and communities and has a significant impact on property values. The research paper further explains that the results are robust and not affected by other observable factors such as economic shocks.'

'The study also says that the benefits of reducing pollution may not be the same in all communities,' Ian added. 'People in areas with higher pollution levels may not value clean air as much as people in cleaner areas.'

Sarah furrowed her brow, seeking clarification. 'What do you mean by "may not value clean air as much?"'

'Well, the paper suggests that people who live in areas with more pollution may have already adjusted to it and don't perceive it as a significant problem,' Ian replied. 'So, if you reduce pollution in those areas, it may not have as much of an impact on property values or quality of life as it would in areas with less pollution.'

Sarah nodded thoughtfully, 'That makes sense. But what about the economic benefits of reducing air pollution? Did the study find any?'

Ian smiled, 'Yes, actually. The authors conducted a benefit analysis to investigate the economic benefits of the regulations. They estimated the willingness to pay (WTP) for air quality improvements and found that the WTP for the late 1970s reductions in TSPs is approximately $45 billion, which is also an estimate of the increase in local property values attributable to the regulation.'

Sarah raised her eyebrows in surprise, 'Wow, that's a significant amount. So, the regulation had both economic and social benefits?'

Ian nodded, 'Yes, exactly. It's worth noting though that the convention for calculating the value of a one-unit decline in TSPs may be flawed.'

Sarah looked confused, 'What do you mean?'

Ian explained, 'Well, the assumption that the entire increase in housing prices is due to the change in air quality as of 1980 may not be entirely realistic. People's expectations about future air quality may have also played a role in the increase in housing prices. So, the authors made two alternative calculations that account for expectations and the long-lived nature of housing assets, and the results remained unchanged.'

Sarah nodded, 'I see. It's important to consider all factors when assessing the impact of air pollution on property values.'

Ian smiled, 'Exactly. This research provides valuable insights for local governments and policymakers, as they can now have a monetary measure to determine the success of their policies in reducing air pollution and promoting clean air.'

'That's interesting,' Sarah remarked, pausing to consider before asking, 'I wonder if air pollution affects the land market in the same way it does the housing market?'

Ian looked up from his iPad, intrigued by Sarah's question. 'Hmm, that's an interesting question, Sarah. I remember reading some related papers on this topic. Let me look them up for you.' He quickly searched for the papers and found two that were related to the effect of air pollution on the land market.

'According to this study, there is indeed evidence that air pollution affects not just the housing market, but the land market as well,' said Ian.

Sarah leaned forward, intrigued. 'How so?'

Ian continued, 'The authors argue that air pollution could lead to a decrease in investors' cognitive abilities, which could then affect land valuation and lead to lower transaction prices. They tested this hypothesis by looking at land transactions in Beijing, and they found that air pollution does indeed have a negative impact on land prices.'

There are three main methods used for transacting land in China, which include auctions, bilateral agreements (Xieyi), and government transfers (Huabo). Among the auction methods, Paimai and Guapai are the most commonly used, and Zhaobiao is an invitation-based auction for qualified bidders. Xieyi involves one-on-one negotiations with the local government, while Huabo refers to a government transfer. In the primary land market, the government has the executive power to manage land supply, which strongly influences market outcomes. To establish a 'healthy' land market, the central government initiated a significant market-oriented land reform in the early 2000s, requiring lands for business operations to be transacted through public auctions.

Huang and Du (2022) conducted a study that analysed data on land transactions between 2007 and 2016 in twenty-nine cities across six provinces. The researchers used various transaction-level attributes, including transaction price, buyers' identity, land area, address, land class, proposed usage, and transaction method. The study's sample size was 89,102 transaction records, and the researchers applied certain restrictions such as excluding incomplete observations, direct government transfers, and Winsorizing the unit price at the 2 per cent level to mitigate the influence of outliers on the results. The study shows that air pollution has a substantial impact on investor behaviour and the prices of transacted land. The effects are statistically and economically significant, with a 1.6 per cent reduction in land prices observed for every 100 unit increase in ambient air pollution in the baseline estimation. Exposure to higher levels of air pollution results in lower bidding prices and price premiums for land among real estate investors.

'Tell me, Ian,' Sarah said, 'what are the underlying mechanisms through which air pollution affects land transactions?'

Ian leaned back in his chair, a thoughtful look on his face. 'There are a couple of theories,' he said, 'but one that's been getting a lot of attention lately is salience theory.'

'Salience theory?' Sarah asked, raising an eyebrow.

'Yes,' Ian replied. 'It suggests that decision makers pay more attention to certain features that stand out and affect decision-making. In the case of air pollution and land demand, high air pollution causes people to focus on the risk of real estate development and lowers the perceived value of land.'

Sarah nodded, taking notes as Ian continued. 'Another theory is projection bias,' he said. 'This is the tendency among people to rely too heavily on their present state of mind and to project their current beliefs and preferences onto the future, resulting in biased decisions.'

'Interesting,' Sarah said, 'so how do these theories affect land transactions?'

'Well,' Ian said, 'The current state of air pollution can affect an investor's expectations of future profits from land purchased for housing development, leading to changes in demand and willingness to purchase land.'

Sarah leaned forward in her seat, her eyes widening with interest. 'But can people learn to correct their biases?' she asked Ian.

Ian nodded. 'That's exactly what the researchers looked at. They wanted to see if buyers' experiences could help them to attenuate the effect of air pollution on land prices.'

Sarah furrowed her brow in confusion. 'Attenuate? What does that mean?'

Ian chuckled. 'Sorry, I mean that they wanted to see if buyers' experiences could lessen the negative impact of air pollution on land prices.'

Sarah nodded, understanding. 'And what did they find?'

Ian smiled. 'They found that buyers' experiences can indeed attenuate the effect of air pollution on land prices, which further supports the projection bias hypothesis.'

'Interesting. Is there anything else we should consider?' asked Sarah.

'Well, another potential mechanism is risk aversion,' Ian explained. 'Investors may perceive polluted environments to be riskier, which could lead to a decrease in demand for land in those areas.'

The risk aversion hypothesis proposes that the decline in land prices due to air pollution could be explained by investors' heightened sense of risk. To investigate this possibility, Huang and Du (2022) utilized the hedonic price model to evaluate the impact of air pollution on land prices, while accounting for several property characteristics, including size, location, and age. The findings revealed that air pollution has a considerable unfavourable effect on land prices, even after accounting for property features, indicating that the influence of air pollution on land prices is not solely determined by property characteristics. In addition, to further examine the risk aversion hypothesis, the study evaluated the influence of air pollution on the pricing of risky assets, such as stocks, using the event study method. The results showed that air pollution had a significant negative impact on the stock prices of firms in the construction and real estate sectors, indicating that investors perceive these industries as riskier in polluted environments.

Sarah was fascinated by the research and asked, 'So does this mean that mood and risk aversion can also explain the negative effect of air pollution on land prices?'

'Yes, that's right,' Ian confirmed. 'However, the exact mechanism may vary depending on the context and the type of investors involved. This effect is stronger for high unit price land and private real estate developers, and is consistent with the projection bias hypothesis, suggesting that exposure to air pollution can impact cognition, mood, and risk attitudes.'

Sarah nodded, trying to grasp the implications of Ian's explanation. 'So, if air pollution affects the perception of risk, then wouldn't that mean that investors would demand a higher return for investing in polluted environments?'

'Exactly,' Ian replied. 'The study implies that air pollution has non-negligible impacts on the land market, and policy makers should consider the influence of air pollution on investors' demand for land and transacted land prices when regulating land trade market. The negative effect of air pollution on land prices indicates the economic cost of air pollution and some degree of market inefficiency, and the benefit of environmental policy for mitigating air pollution would be capitalized into land values.'

Sarah's curiosity was piqued as she noticed a particular paper that caught her attention. 'What's that one?' she asked, leaning in to peer at Ian's screen and pointing to the paper of interest.

'Oh, this one is by Pan et al. (2022). It's another study on the same topic, but they seem to have taken a different approach,' Ian explained.

'Really? How is it different?' Sarah asked curiously.

Ian scrolled through the paper, searching for the relevant section. 'Here it is. The authors examine the consequences of acquiring land during the winter in China, and how it relates to air pollution. But there are some differences in their approach and mechanisms. For instance, Huang and Du (2022) focused on the channels of projection bias, mood, and risk aversion, while Pan et al. (2022) also looked at salience bias and learning behaviour.' Ian explained.

'I see. So, they're looking at a different aspect of the same problem. That's interesting,' Sarah remarked.

'Yes, exactly. It's always good to see how other researchers are approaching the same topic. We can learn a lot from their methodology and findings,' Ian replied.

'Can you tell me more about it?' asked Sarah.

'The researchers wanted to find out if having access to heating services affected the price of land in a city. They used a method called the "hedonic pricing model", which is a way of figuring out how much a property is worth based on its characteristics. They compared land prices in the cities above and below the Qinling–Huai River line before and after the provision of the heating service. You know what the Qinling–Huai River line is, right?' Ian turned to Sarah.

'Ah, the Qinling–Huai River line—it's like a magic border that separates the chilly north from the slightly warmer south in China. You see, if your property is north of this line, you're in luck because you get heating service to keep you cozy during the cold months. But if your property is south of the line, well, you're on your own and have to find other ways to stay warm!' Sarah explained with a hint of amusement in her tone.

Ian elaborated, 'They found that land parcels in the south are sold at lower prices in the winter than in the non-winter seasons, due to buyers' cognitive bias. But what's more interesting is that they looked at a subsample of buyers who engaged in multiple transactions and found that individuals in non-heating cities, through their repeated purchase activities, learn from the market mispricing. They're actually more likely to choose winter as the time of transactions as their experience increases.'

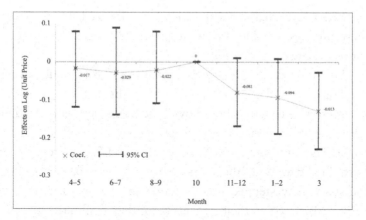

Figure 8.2: Unit-price differences between non-heating
and heating cities, by calendar period

Source: Pan, Y., Qin, Y., Zhang, F., and Zhu, H. (2022). 'Acquiring land
in cold winter: Consequences and possible explanations.' *Journal of
Environmental Economics and Management*, 116, 102721.

Sarah raised an eyebrow. 'That's fascinating. It raises a lot of
questions about how people make decisions, especially high-value
products like land parcels. Do you think this learning effect could
be generalized to other types of purchases?'

Ian considered Sarah's question for a moment before
answering, 'It's hard to say, but it's definitely worth exploring. The
researchers also found that the decision to purchase land parcels
is never a small issue for buyers, so understanding the factors that
influence their decision-making process could have significant
implications.'

Sarah's eyes sparkled with curiosity as she asked, 'Do you think these findings could lead to more informed policies or strategies for real estate development?'

Ian nodded in agreement. 'And it's not just about buyers' decisions, it could also have an impact on the market as a whole. It's interesting to think about how these cognitive biases could be corrected over time and what effect that could have on land prices.'

As they finished their breakfast, Ian and Sarah prepared to start their day. With their minds buzzing with thoughts from the study, they stepped out the door and began their walk to work. Engrossed in their conversation, they continued to delve into the implications of air pollution on the housing market. The implications of air pollution on the housing market had given them plenty to think about, but they were determined to find ways to use the research to improve the lives of those in their community.

Chapter 9

Catch Me If You Can: The Surprising Link Between Air Pollution and Criminal Behaviour

Ian and Sarah were sitting at their kitchen table, enjoying their morning coffee. Ian was reading the news on his phone when he came across a headline that caught his attention.

'Hey, Sarah, did you remember last week we talked about the train derailment in Ohio?' he asked, turning his phone towards her. Sarah nodded in response.

Ian continued, 'Well, it seems like there's been more trouble in that area. According to the news, there have been multiple bank robberies in the same counties affected by the train derailment, with three of them happening after the incident.'

Sarah furrowed her brows, 'That's terrible. I hope nobody got hurt.'

'The police are saying that the robbers got away with over $100,000 in cash,' Ian said, shaking his head. 'It's hard to believe that people would resort to such violent acts.'

Sarah nodded in agreement. 'It's a sad reflection of the state of our society. I wonder if there's anything we can do to address the root causes of crime like this.'

Ian shrugged. 'I don't know. It's a complex issue. Poverty, inequality, lack of opportunity, mental health problems . . . all of these factors can contribute to criminal behaviour.'

'But what does it have to do with the train derailment?' Sarah asked.

Ian shrugged, 'I don't know, but it made me wonder if there's a possible link between air pollution and criminal activity.'

Sarah took a thoughtful sip of her coffee. 'Really? How so?'

'Well,' Ian explained, 'there have been studies showing that air pollution can have negative effects on people's health and behaviour. It's possible that the toxic chemicals released during the train derailment could have had a similar effect on the people living in the area, causing them to engage in more violent or criminal activities.'

Sarah pondered over Ian's theory, 'That's definitely an interesting thought. It's worth looking into more, especially with the recent bank robberies.' Ian nodded in agreement, emphasizing the need to consider all possible factors when it comes to crime prevention and environmental safety.

As they finished their coffee, Ian and Sarah sat at their computer, eager to find out more about the possible link between air pollution and criminal activity. They scoured the internet, digging up research studies, news articles, and even local crime reports to gain a better understanding of the situation.

Ian scrolled through pages of scientific journals, analysing the data and statistics presented in each article. Meanwhile, Sarah combed through news reports, looking for any patterns or trends that could provide insight into the recent bank robberies and their potential connection to the train derailment.

As they worked together, Ian and Sarah began to notice a few key findings. Several studies had indeed shown a correlation between air pollution and aggressive behaviour, with exposure to toxins leading to increased crime rates in certain areas. In addition, the news reports revealed a stark increase in violent crimes within the Ohio counties affected by the train derailment.

Air pollution is a critical problem in today's society, receiving global attention due to its adverse effects on health outcomes. Extensive research has established a strong link between exposure to air pollution and chronic diseases, respiratory issues, and mortality. Additionally, short-term exposure to pollution has been linked to cognitive skill development, anxiety, and aggressive or criminal behaviour. Despite growing concerns, few studies have attempted to identify the relationship between air pollution exposure and criminal activity.

'I just read a really interesting paper about air pollution and criminal activity in Chicago,' Ian said. 'It's called "Air Pollution and Criminal Activity: Microgeographic Evidence from Chicago" and it was published in the *American Economic Journal: Applied Economics*.'

Sarah looked intrigued and asked, 'What's it about?'

Ian explained, 'Well, the study uses wind direction as an instrument for pollution to investigate the relationship between air pollution and crime in Chicago. And get this—they discovered that air pollution is linked to an increase in violent crime, but it doesn't seem to have the same effect on property crime. This aligns with other research that has found a connection between air pollution and aggressive behaviour.'

Sarah leaned in and asked, 'How did they conduct the study?'

'Here's the really interesting part,' Ian continued, eager to share the findings from the study. 'They looked closely at the way pollution and crime are distributed across Chicago and focused on five major highways that run through the city. By comparing crime rates on opposite sides of these highways on days when the wind was blowing in a certain direction, they were able to estimate the impact of pollution on criminal activity. And you know what they found? On the downwind side of the highways, violent crime increased by almost 2 per cent! But get this, there was no effect on property crime. It's crazy to think about how something like pollution could have such a big impact on the safety of a community.'

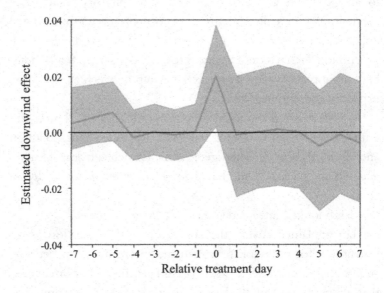

Figure 9.1: Leading and lagging downwind treatment effects

Source: Herrnstadt, E., Heyes, A., Muehlegger, E., and Saberian, S. (2021). 'Air pollution and criminal activity: Microgeographic evidence from Chicago.' *American Economic Journal: Applied Economics*, 13(4), 70–100.

Sarah's eyes widened with intrigue as she asked Ian, 'Did they perform any additional tests to confirm that pollution is indeed the driving mechanism behind the increase in crime?'

Ian nodded thoughtfully and said, 'It's actually quite interesting. The study found that the impact of pollution was weaker on days when the wind didn't blow it in a specific direction, spreading it more evenly. And get this—the closer you are to the pollution source, the stronger the effect on crime. But what's even more intriguing is that the effect was most pronounced on days with moderate temperatures; when people tend to spend more time outside and are therefore more vulnerable to pollution exposure. Fascinating, isn't it?'

Research in medicine, biology, and psychology has uncovered several possible ways in which pollution exposure might increase aggression in people. One way is that pollution can cause physical discomfort, which has been linked to aggressive behaviour in many studies (Anderson and Bushman, 2002; Rotton, 1983; Rotton et al., 1978). In fact, exposure to bad smells in the lab has been shown to reduce cognitive performance, tolerance for frustration, and even ratings of other people and the environment (Rotton, 1983; Rotton et al., 1978). Another pathway linking pollution and aggression is through brain chemistry. Air pollution may directly lower levels of serotonin, a neurotransmitter that helps inhibit aggression, and this has been linked to increased impulsivity and aggression in both children and adults. Third, air pollutants can inflame nerve tissues in humans and animals, leading to increased aggression. Finally, pollution can cause other physiological changes that increase aggression, such as elevated levels of testosterone, which has been linked to violent crime.

Sarah nodded and asked, 'What about the placebo tests?'

Ian explained, 'The researchers created thirty "fake" interstates that were parallel to the actual interstate they studied and conducted tests on those. They discovered that the downwind treatment effect was highest at the same latitude where the interstate crosses Chicago. Additionally, they employed another method to test their findings, where they compared the sides of the interstates to each other, on the same day of the year, but in different years with either more or less downwind exposure. Interestingly, they obtained similar results and concluded that air pollution indeed leads to a rise in violent crime, but not property crime.'

Sarah was impressed and remarked, 'This study is captivating! It helps us understand the link between air pollution and crime and offers valuable insights for policymakers looking to reduce air pollution in urban areas.'

Ian nodded and said, 'Yes, and the fact that they used microgeographic data to conduct the study makes it more convincing. It's amazing how data can help us understand the world around us better.'

Sarah agreed and said, 'It's exciting to see how data can be used to inform policy decisions and make a real impact on people's lives.'

'Hey, have you heard about the NBP?' Sarah added, she'd found an interesting research paper on her tablet.

'No, I haven't. What's it about?' replied Ian, intrigued.

'The NBP was a cap-and-trade system that aimed to reduce ozone concentrations in the eastern and midwestern states of the US, including Washington DC. It was initiated in 2003 and ended in 2008, and only operated from May to September because ozone concentrations were generally high in the summer,' Sarah said, explaining the background of the paper she read.

The Nitrogen Oxides Budget Trading Program (NBP) was a cap-and-trade market established in the United States to control NOx emissions in the eastern states. The programme was initiated by the Ozone Transport Commission (OTC) in response to the high ozone levels in northeast regions caused by the transportation of NOx from the industrial Midwest to the northeast. The market operated from May to September, covering eight northeastern states and Washington, D.C., with an additional eleven states joining the programme in 2004. The programme included 2,500 electricity generating units and industrial boilers, among which 700 coal-fired plants produced around 95 per cent of NOx emissions. Each state received a set of permits and determined how to distribute them to regulated sources, which could trade them through open markets. The EPA allocated approximately 150,000 tons of NOx allowances in 2003, 650,000 tons in 2004, and around 550,000 tons each year from 2005 to 2008. Regulated sources were allowed to bank allowances for future years, and any unused allowances were saved for subsequent years (Sun et al., 2020).

The NBP emission market significantly reduced NOx emissions, especially in counties with high NOx emissions levels. The programme's impact on crime was investigated by scholars to study the association between air pollution and crime rates. The scholars used the NBP as an exogenous shock and found that a 10 per cent reduction in NOx emissions led to a 4 per cent reduction in violent crime and a 2 per cent reduction in property crime (Chen et al., 2019). The study provides evidence of the potential social benefits of environmental policies aimed at reducing air pollution. However, the study also highlights the need for further research to explore the long-term effects of the NBP and similar programmes on crime rates and other social outcomes. Overall, the NBP emission market was a successful environmental policy that significantly reduced NOx emissions in the eastern United States and had positive social implications (Sun et al., 2020; Chen et al., 2019).

Ian looked interested and asked, 'What's the connection between the NBP and this research paper?'

'Well, this paper investigates the impact of the NBP on crime rates,' Sarah replied. 'By compiling county-season-level crime data with air pollution and weather information, the study found that the NBP market significantly lowered violent crime rates in participating states by 3.7 per cent. To put this figure into perspective, the effect of the NBP on violent crimes is equivalent to increasing the size of police forces by approximately 9 per cent during the sample period.'

'That's interesting. How did they come up with this conclusion?' Ian asked.

'They used a triple-difference framework to examine the relationship between air pollution and criminal activities.

The quasi-experiment provides three dimensions of variations. The first is the difference in criminal activities between NBP and non-NBP states. The second difference is determined from comparisons in values measured before and after the market's initiation. The last difference is identified from a comparison of summer and winter values,' Sarah explained.

Ian was impressed and asked Sarah to share more about the findings. Sarah pulled out her phone and quickly accessed the research data. 'Specifically, rates for assault, robbery, rape, and murder decreased by 2.5 per cent, 7.9 per cent, 6.6 per cent, and 6.8 per cent respectively. The NBP's effects on property crimes are slightly less significant, with the NBP market reducing property crime rate in participating states by 2.9 per cent. Rates for larceny and burglary fell by 3.3 per cent and 2.9 per cent respectively. However, the NBP's effect on motor vehicle theft is not statistically significant at the traditional level.'

Ian was curious about whether the triple-difference estimator method was reliable, so he asked Sarah how the researchers made sure their assumptions were valid. Sarah explained that the researchers used three methods to examine whether any trends existed before the intervention started. First, they created graphs to see how criminal activity changed over time in states that implemented the new policy and those that didn't. They found that there were no significant differences in criminal activity before the policy was introduced, which suggested that any changes in criminal activity after the policy was implemented could be attributed to the new policy. Second, they compared the linear trends in criminal activity in states that implemented the policy with those that didn't. They found no clear differences in trends, which again supported the idea that the changes in criminal activity were likely caused by the new policy and not some pre-existing trend. Finally, they conducted a falsification test by introducing a fake policy and looking at the effects on criminal activity.

They found that there were no changes in criminal activity during this fake policy period, which suggested that any changes seen during the actual policy period were indeed caused by the new policy and not some other factor. Overall, these three methods helped the researchers confirm that the changes in criminal activity they observed were likely caused by the new policy, and not some pre-existing trend.

'That's really cool! Did the researchers have any other ways to figure out if air pollution affects crime?' Ian asked excitedly.

'Definitely! They used another approach called the instrumental variable (IV) method to see if air pollution measured by the air quality index had an impact on crime rates. And guess what? The results showed that air pollution has a significant effect on violent and property crime. Compared to the fixed-effect method, the IV method helps to account for variables that weren't included before and minimizes errors in the estimates,' Sarah explained.

Ian looked thoughtful and asked, 'What about the effects of the NBP on other economic indicators?'

'The researchers found that the NBP has no impact on unemployment rates, worker earnings, or electricity demand, validating the exclusion restriction assumption of the IV approach,' Sarah replied.

Ian was amazed by the thoroughness of the researchers and asked if they conducted any additional tests to validate their results.

Sarah replied, 'Yes, they did. First, they examined the heterogeneous effect of the NBP by looking at NOx emissions recorded before the NBP. They found that the NBP effects on crimes were mainly driven by counties with high NOx emission levels. Second, they simultaneously tested multiple hypotheses to make their inferences more conservative, and the inferences of their main results remained stable. Finally, they investigated whether their results were robust to excluding adjacent states by randomly assigning them to treatment or control groups.

The results of the robustness checks showed that their main findings remained robust, indicating that their results were not driven by neighbouring states that were affected by the NBP.'

Ian was impressed by the attention to detail and commitment of the researchers to ensure that their findings were accurate and not just a coincidence. 'It's amazing to see how much effort they put into ensuring that their results were valid,' he commented, pointing to another research paper. 'Here is another interesting study I found.'

'What's it all about?' Sarah replied, curious.

Ian began to explain. 'Well, the study used a unique method to investigate the effect of short-term exposure to air pollution on aggressive behaviour at a national scale. They combined two highly detailed datasets—one on criminal activity and another on daily-county level air pollution. They found that a 10 per cent increase in same-day exposure to PM2.5 is associated with a 0.14 per cent increase in violent crimes, nearly all of which is driven by increases in assaults.'

Ian added. 'And it's not just PM2.5. They also found that a 10 per cent increase in same-day exposure to ozone is associated with a 0.3 per cent increase in violent crime or a 0.35 per cent increase in assaults. The results are pretty robust too, they tested it against a battery of alternative specifications and weather conditions.'

Sarah listened intently. 'That's fascinating. So, the social cost of pollution is not just long-term health effects, but it also has an impact on crime rates?' she asked.

'Exactly,' Ian nodded. 'It seems that aggressive behaviour is a key social cost of pollution that has been absent from policy discussions. The study also found that the effects of PM2.5 are largest at lower temperatures while the effects of ozone are largest at relatively higher temperatures.'

Sarah was intrigued. 'Wow, that's a crucial piece of information. I wonder if policymakers are aware of this. It seems like reducing daily PM2.5 or ozone by only 10 per cent will save a lot of money in crime costs per year.'

Ian nodded in agreement. 'Yes, the study estimates that it will save $405 million to $1 billion in crime costs per year via reduced assaults. That's a significant amount of money that can be used for other purposes.'

Sarah was thoughtful for a moment. 'This research highlights the importance of investing in policies that reduce air pollution. It's not just about improving our health, but it also has a direct impact on our safety and the safety of our communities.'

Ian agreed. 'Absolutely. I think this study has significant implications for future research and policy. It suggests that there are important but understudied effects of pollution beyond long-term health effects, and the extent of our understanding of the social costs of pollution may be limited by the current scope of research.'

Burkhardt et al. (2020) discusses the potential physiological pathways that may drive the observed association between short-term exposure to air pollution and aggressive behaviour. Research in epidemiology and public health that can offer insight into several plausible mechanisms. For instance, environmental pollutants, such as fine particulate matter air pollution, can initiate biological processes that lead to systemic inflammation, which is linked to both chronic and short-term health responses, including respiratory problems (Brook et al., 2004; Donaldson et al., 2001).

Research has also shown that short-term changes in systemic inflammation can exacerbate cognitive and motor symptoms of disease and accelerate disease progression (Cunningham et al., 2009). Therefore, it is plausible that similar biochemical and biological mechanisms underlie aggressive behaviour, and that transient ambient air pollution levels could be associated with an increased propensity for aggressive behaviour.

Furthermore, there is evidence to suggest that acute changes in air pollution may interact with psychological factors, such as perceived control, coping resources, impulsiveness, and certain personality traits, which may mediate the influence of physical environmental stressors (Lu et al., 2018; Power et al., 2015; Sass et al., 2017). These findings suggest that further research on the effects of transient air pollution exposures on cognitive and behavioural outcomes, particularly aggressive behaviour, is warranted.

'It's interesting to see the link between air pollution and crime in the US. But have you found any evidence from other countries?' Sarah asked, 'most of the research I've seen has been focused on the US. But it would be interesting to see if the relationship holds true in other countries as well.'

Ian nodded. 'Actually, there's a study I came across that looked at this question in the UK. It's called "Crime is in the air: The contemporaneous relationship between air pollution and crime," by Bondy, Roth, and Sager. They found that air pollution is positively associated with both property and violent crime in London.'

Sarah looked surprised. 'That's really interesting. Do they say anything about why air pollution might be linked to crime?'

Ian opened up his laptop and pulled up the study by Bondy et al. (2020). 'According to their findings, air pollution could lead to cognitive impairment, reduced mental well-being, and greater levels of aggression and violence,' he explained. 'All of these factors could contribute to higher rates of crime in areas with high levels of air pollution.'

In England and Wales, the total cost of crime is estimated to be around £60 billion per year, according to the UK government. This suggests that effective crime reduction measures can result in substantial savings. Meanwhile, epidemiology and economic literature have demonstrated the adverse effects of ambient air pollution on many aspects of human health and life. However, evidence on the link between pollution and crime is very scarce.

To address this gap, a study was conducted by Bondy, Roth, and Sager (2020) in London, utilizing high-quality daily administrative crime data in conjunction with an extensive network of air pollution monitoring stations. The study investigated whether short-term exposure to elevated levels of ambient air pollution affects crime rates in the city. The findings build on previous research by Lu et al. (2018), Li (2017), Zou (2018), and Herrnstadt et al. (2018).

The results of the study suggest that mitigating air pollution in urban areas may serve as an effective strategy for reducing crime rates. The observed correlation between pollution and criminal activity implies that incorporating pollution forecasts into the allocation of law enforcement resources could prove beneficial. Moreover, the study demonstrates that pollution levels below the current standards set by the US EPA and the UK Department for Environment, Food and Rural Affairs (DEFRA) still exhibit significant impacts, highlighting the potential economic benefits of revising these guidelines.

Sarah nodded thoughtfully. 'That makes sense. But do you think the same mechanism applies to different types of crime?'

Ian brought up another study on his laptop, this one by Singh et al. (2020), which examined the relationship between air pollution and property crime in India. 'Interestingly, this study found that air pollution may increase economic stress, which could in turn increase the incentive for property crimes like theft and burglary.'

Sarah was intrigued. 'So, air pollution could have different effects on different types of crime, depending on the context.'

Ian nodded. 'Exactly. And the more we understand about these relationships, the better equipped we'll be to develop effective policies and interventions that can reduce crime rates and improve public health in areas with high levels of air pollution.'

Sarah smiled. 'It's amazing how research can shed light on issues that we may not have considered before. I hope policymakers take note of this and implement policies that prioritize reducing air pollution.' Ian continued, 'And not just for the sake of reducing crime costs, but also for the health and well-being of our communities. It's sobering to think about the millions of deaths attributed to exposure to PM2.5 alone, and the fact that these effects extend beyond just physical health. This study is a wake-up call to take air pollution seriously and invest in solutions that can mitigate its harmful effects.'

Sarah nodded in agreement. 'Absolutely, and it's not just up to policymakers. We can all take steps to reduce our own contribution to air pollution, like using public transportation or biking instead of driving, and supporting businesses that prioritize sustainability. We all have a responsibility to do our part.'

Ian smiled, grateful for his wife's passion for the environment. 'You're right, and I'm glad we can have these conversations and take action together.'

As they finished their coffee, Ian and Sarah continued to discuss the implications of the study and brainstorm ways they could make a positive impact in their community. Both of them felt inspired to make a difference and hopeful for a future with cleaner air and safer communities.

Acknowledgements

Yang gratefully acknowledges the support from the Research Grants Council of Hong Kong (Grant No: 14504022) and the National Natural Science Foundation of China (Grant No: 72203192). Wang gratefully acknowledges support from the National Natural Science Foundation of China (Grant No: 72303035).

References

Agarwal, S., Han, Y., Qin, Y., and Zhu, H. (2023). 'Disguised pollution: Industrial activities in the dark.' *Journal of Public Economics*, 223. https://doi.org/10.1016/j.jpubeco.2023.104904 (accessed October 20, 2023).

Agarwal, S., Sing, T.F., and Yang, Y. (2020). 'The impact of transboundary haze pollution on household utilities consumption.' *Energy Economics*, 85.

Agarwal, S., Wang, L., and Yang, Y. (2023). 'Online Consumption Response to Sustained Exposure to Air Pollution: Evidence from a Quasi-experiment in China.' Working Paper.

Alexander, D., and Schwandt, H. (2022). 'The Impact of Car Pollution on Infant and Child Health: Evidence from Emissions Cheating.' *The Review of Economic Studies*, 89(6), 2872–910. https://doi.org/10.1093/restud/rdac007 (accessed October 20, 2023).

Almond, D., Chen, Y., Greenstone, M., and Li, H. (2009). 'Winter Heating or Clean Air? Unintended Impacts of China's Huai River Policy.' *The American Economic Review*, 99(2), 184–190. https://doi.org/10.1257/aer.99.2.184 (accessed October 20, 2023).

Anderson, C.A., and Bushman, B.J. (2002). 'Human aggression.' *Annual Review of Psychology*, 53(1), 27–51.

Auchincloss, A.H., Diez Roux, A.V., Dvonch, J.T., Brown, P.L., Barr, R.G., Daviglus, M.L., . . . & O'Neill, M.S. (2008).

'Associations between recent exposure to ambient fine particulate matter and blood pressure in the Multi-Ethnic Study of Atherosclerosis' (MESA). *Environmental health perspectives*, 116(4), 486–491.

Azar, O.H. (2007). 'Relative thinking theory.' *The Journal of Socio-Economics*, 36(1), 1–14.

Baker, M., and Wurgler, J. (2006). 'Investor sentiment and the cross-section of stock returns.' *The Journal of Finance*, 61(4), 1645–80.

Barber, B.M., and Odean, T. (2000). 'Trading is hazardous to your wealth: The common stock investment performance of individual investors.' *The Journal of Finance*, 55(2), 773–806.

Barber, B.M., and Odean, T. (2001). 'Boys will be boys: Gender, overconfidence, and common stock investment.' *Quarterly Journal of Economics*, 116(1), 261–92.

Beijing Municipal Environmental Monitoring Center. (2021). 'Beijing Municipal Environmental Quality Report 2020.'

Bondy, M., Roth, S., and Sager, L. (2020). 'Crime Is in the Air: The Contemporaneous Relationship between Air Pollution and Crime.' *Journal of the Association of Environmental and Resource Economists*, 7(3), 555–85.

Bordalo, P., Gennaioli, N., and Shleifer, A. (2012). 'Salience theory of choice under risk.' *The Quarterly Journal of Economics*, 127(3), 1243–85.

Bordalo, P., Gennaioli, N., and Shleifer, A. (2013). 'Salience and consumer choice.' *Journal of Political Economy*, 121(5), 803–43.

Bordalo, P., Gennaioli, N., and Shleifer, A. (2013). 'Salience and asset prices.' *American Economic Review*, 103(3), 623–28.

Brook, R. D., Franklin, B., Cascio, W., Hong, Y., Howard, G., Lipsett, M., . . . and Rajagopalan, S. (2004). 'Air pollution and cardiovascular disease: a statement for healthcare professionals from the expert panel on population and prevention science of the American Heart Association.' *Circulation*, 109(21), 2655–71.

Brunekreef, B., and Holgate, S. T. (2002). 'Air pollution and health.' *The Lancet (British Edition)*, 360(9341), 1233–42. https://doi. org/10.1016/S0140-6736(02)11274-8 (accessed October 20, 2023).

Bushong, B., Rabin, M., and Schwartzstein, J. (2021). 'A Model of Relative Thinking.' *The Review of Economic Studies*, 88(1), 162–91.

Busse, M.R., Pope, D.G., Pope, J.C., and Silva-Risso, J. (2015). 'The Psychological Effect of Weather on Car Purchases.' *The Quarterly Journal of Economics*, 130(1), 371–414. https://doi.org/10.1093/qje/qju033 (accessed October 20, 2023).

Cacciottolo, M., Wang, X., Driscoll, I., Woodward, N., Saffari, A., Reyes, J., Serre, M.L., Vizuete, W., Sioutas, C., Morgan, T.E., et al. (2017). 'Particulate air pollutants, APOE alleles and their contributions to cognitive impairment in older women and to amyloidogenesis in experimental models.' *Translational Psychiatry* 7, e1022. DOI: 10.1038/tp.2016.262.

Cao, Z., Zhou, J., Li, M., Huang, J., and Dou, D. (2023). 'Urbanites' mental health undermined by air pollution.' *Nature Sustainability*, 6(4), 470–78. https://doi.org/10.1038/s41893-022-01032-1 (accessed October 20, 2023).

Chang, T.Y., Graff Zivin, J., Gross, T., and Neidell, M. (2019). 'The effect of pollution on worker productivity: evidence from call center workers in China.' *American Economic Journal: Applied Economics*, 11(1), 151–72.

Chang, T.Y., Huang, W., & Wang, Y. (2018). 'Something in the air: Pollution and the Demand for Health Insurance'. *The Review of Economic Studies*, 85(3 (304)), 1609–1634. https:// doi.org/10.1093/restud/rdy016 (accessed October 20, 2023).

Chang, T.Y., Huang, W., and Wang, Y. (2018). 'Something in the Air: Pollution and the Demand for Health Insurance'.

The Review of Economic Studies, 85(3 (304)), 1609–1634. https://
www.jstor.org/stable/26543944 (accessed October 20, 2023).

Chang, T., Graff Zivin, J., Gross, T., and Neidell, M. (2016).
'Particulate pollution and the productivity of pear packers.'
American Economic Journal: Economic Policy, 8(3), 141–69.

Chay, K.Y., and Greenstone, M (2003). 'Air Quality, Infant
Mortality, and the Clean Air Act of 1970.' No. w10053.
National Bureau of Economic Research Working Paper.

Chay, K.Y., and Greenstone, M. (2005). 'Does Air Quality Matter?
Evidence from the Housing Market.' *The Journal of Political
Economy*, 113(2), 376–424.

Chegut, A., Eichholtz, P., and Kok, N. (2014). 'Supply, demand
and the value of green buildings.' *Urban Studies*, 51(1), 22–43.

Chegut, A., Eichholtz, P., and Holtermans, R. (2016). 'Energy
efficiency and economic value in affordable housing.' *Energy
Policy*, 97, 39–49.

Chen, Y., Ebenstein, A., Greenstone, M., and Li, H. (2013).
'Evidence on the impact of sustained exposure to air pollution
on life expectancy from China's Huai River policy.' *Proceedings
of the National Academy of Sciences - PNAS*, 110(32), 12936–
41. https://doi.org/10.1073/pnas.1300018110 (accessed
October 20, 2023).

Cheng, J., Su, J., Cui, T., Li, X., Dong, X., Sun, F., . . . and He, K.
(2019). 'Dominant role of emission reduction in PM 2.5 air
quality improvement in Beijing during 2013–2017: a model-
based decomposition analysis'. *Atmospheric Chemistry and
Physics*, 19(9), 6125-6146.

Clark, C.F., Kotchen, M.J., and Moore, M.R. (2003). 'Internal
and external influences on pro-environmental behavior:
Participation in a green electricity program.' *Journal of
Environmental Psychology*, 23(3), 237–46.

Conlin, M., O'Donoghue, T., and Vogelsang, T.J. (2007). 'Projection
Bias in Catalog Orders.' *The American Economic Review*, 97(4),

1217–49.   https://doi.org/10.1257/000282807783286810 (accessed October 20, 2023).

Cramer-Flood, E. (2021). 'In Global Historic First, Ecommerce in China Will Account for More Than 50% of Retail Sales. eMarketer (February 10).' https://www.emarketer.com/content/global-historic-first-ecommerce-china-will-account-more-than-50-of-retail-sales (accessed October 20, 2023).

Currie, J., Zivin, J. G., Mullins, J., and Neidell, M. (2014). 'What Do We Know About Short- and Long-Term Effects of Early-Life Exposure to Pollution?' *Annual Review of Resource Economics*, 6(1), 217–47. https://doi.org/10.1146/annurev-resource-100913-012610 (accessed October 20, 2023).

Deng, Y., Li, Z., and Quigley, J.M. (2012). 'Economic returns to energy-efficient investments in the housing market: evidence from Singapore.' *Regional Science and Urban Economics*, 42(3), 506–15.

Dessaint, O., and Matray, A. (2017). 'Do managers overreact to salient risks? Evidence from hurricane strikes.' *Journal of Financial Economics*, 126(1), 97–121.

Devine, A., and Kok, N. (2015). 'Green certification and building performance: Implications for tangibles and intangibles.' *Journal of Portfolio Management*, 41(6), 151–63.

Dhar, R., and Zhu, N. (2006). 'Up close and personal: investor sophistication and the disposition effect.' *Management Science*, 52(5), 726–40.

Dockery, D.W., Pope, C.A., Xu, X., Spengler, J.D., Ware, J.H., Fay, M.E., . . . and Speizer, F.E. (1993). 'An association between air pollution and mortality in six US cities.' *New England Journal of Medicine*, 329(24), 1753–59.

Dockery, D.W., Pope, C.A., Xu, X., Spengler, J.D., Ware, J.H., Fay, M.E., Ferris, B.G., and Speizer, F.E. (1993). 'An Association between Air Pollution and Mortality in Six U.S. Cities.' *The New England Journal of Medicine*, 329(24), 1753–59. https://doi.org/10.1056/NEJM199312093292401 (accessed October 20, 2023).

Donaldson, K., Stone, V., Borm, P.J., Jimenez, L.A., Gilmour, P.S., Schins, R.P., . . . and Tran, C.L. (2001). 'Oxidative stress and calcium signaling in the adverse effects of environmental particles (PM10).' *Free Radical Biology and Medicine*, 31(3), 351–56.

Dong, R., Fisman, R., Wang, Y., and Xu, N. (2021). 'Air pollution, affect, and forecasting bias: Evidence from Chinese financial analysts.' *Journal of Financial Economics*, 139(3), 971–84.

Ebenstein, A., Fan, M., Greenstone, M., He, G., and Zhou, M. (2017). 'New evidence on the impact of sustained exposure to air pollution on life expectancy from China's Huai River Policy.' *Proceedings of the National Academy of Sciences - PNAS*, 114(39), 10384–89. https://doi.org/10.1073/pnas.1616784114 (accessed October 20, 2023).

Ebenstein, A., Fan, M., Greenstone, M., He, G., Yin, P., and Zhou, M. (2015). 'Growth, Pollution, and Life Expectancy: China from 1991-2012.' *The American Economic Review*, 105(5), 226–31. https://doi.org/10.1257/aer.p20151094 (accessed October 20, 2023).

Ebenstein, A., Lavy, V., and Roth, S. (2016). 'The long-run economic consequences of high-stakes examinations: Evidence from transitory variation in pollution'. *American Economic Journal: Applied Economics*, 8(4), 36–65.

Eichholtz, P., Kok, N., and Quigley, J.M. (2010). 'Doing well by doing good? Green office buildings.' *American Economic Review*, 100(5), 2492–509.

Eichholtz, P., Kok, N., and Quigley, J. M. (2013). 'The economics of green building.' *Review of Economics and Statistics*, 95(1), 50–63.

Fuerst, F., McAllister, P., Nanda, A., and Wyatt, P. (2015). 'Does energy efficiency matter to home-buyers? An investigation of EPC ratings and transaction prices in England.' *Energy Economics*, 48, 145–56.

Gan, W.Q., Allen, R.W., Brauer, M., Davies, H.W., Mancini, G.B.J., Lear, S.A., and Chow, C.K. (2019). 'Long-term exposure to traffic-related air pollution and risk of coronary heart disease and stroke: A systematic review and meta-analysis.' *Environmental Health Perspectives*, 127, 077008. DOI: 10.1289/EHP504.

Gauderman, W.J., Urman, R., Avol, E., Berhane, K., McConnell, R., Rappaport, E., Chang, R., Lurmann, F., and Gilliland, F. (2015). 'Association of Improved Air Quality with Lung Development in Children.' *The New England Journal of Medicine*, 372(10), 905–13. https://doi.org/10.1056/NEJ Moa1414123 (accessed October 20, 2023).

Greenstone, M. (2004). 'Did the Clean Air Act cause the remarkable decline in sulphur dioxide concentrations?' *Journal of Environmental Economics and Management*, 47(3), 585–611.

Hastings, J. S., and Shapiro, J. M. (2013). 'Fungibility and consumer choice: Evidence from commodity price shocks.' *The Quarterly Journal of Economics*, 128(4), 1449–98.

Herrnstadt, E., and Muehlegger, E. (2015). 'Air pollution and criminal activity: Evidence from Chicago microdata' (No. w21787). *National Bureau of Economic Research Working Paper*.

Herrnstadt, E., Heyes, A., Muehlegger, E., and Saberian, S. (2021). 'Air pollution and criminal activity: Microgeographic evidence from Chicago.' *American Economic Journal: Applied Economics*, 13(4), 70–100.

Heyes, A., Neidell, M., and Saberian, S. (2016). 'The effect of air pollution on investor behavior: Evidence from the S&P 500 (No. w22753).' *National Bureau of Economic Research Working Paper*.

Huang, J., Xu, N., and Yu, H. (2020). 'Pollution and performance: Do investors make worse trades on hazy days?' *Management Science*, 66(10), 4455–76.

Huang, Z., and Du, X. (2022). 'Does air pollution affect investor cognition and land valuation? Evidence from the Chinese land market.' *Real Estate Economics*, 50(2), 593–613.

International Energy Agency. (2021, December). 'Renewables 2021: Analysis and forecast to 2026.' *IEA.* https://www.iea.org/reports/renewables-2021 (accessed October 20, 2023).

Ito, K., and Zhang, S. (2020). 'Willingness to Pay for Clean Air: Evidence from Air Purifier Markets in China.' *The Journal of Political Economy,* 128(5), 1627 72. https.//doi.org/10.1086/705554 (accessed October 20, 2023).

Jayachandran, S. (2009). 'Air quality and early-life mortality evidence from Indonesia's wildfires.' *Journal of Human Resources,* 44(4), 916–54.

Kahn, M.E., and Kok, N. (2014). 'The capitalization of green labels in the California housing market.' *Regional Science and Urban Economics,* 47, 25–34.

Kahneman, D., and Tversky, A. (1972). 'Subjective probability: A judgment of representativeness.' *Cognitive Psychology,* 3(3), 430–54.

Karplus, V.J., and Wu, M. (2019). 'Smoke and Mirrors: Did China's Environmental Crackdowns Lead to Persistent Changes in Polluting Firm Behavior.' *Alliance for Research on Corporate Sustainability.* https://corporate-sustainability.org/wp-content/uploads/Smoke-and-Mirros.pdf (accessed October 20, 2023).

Karplus, V. J., Zhang, S., and Almond, D. (2018). 'Quantifying coal power plant responses to tighter SO_2 emissions standards in China.' *Proceedings of the National Academy of Sciences,* 115(27), 700–09. https://doi.org/10.1073/pnas.1800605115 (accessed October 20, 2023).

Kingsley, B. S. (2008). 'Making it easy to be green: using impact fees to encourage green building.' *NYUL Rev., 83,* 532.

Kollmuss, A., and Agyeman, J. (2002). 'Mind the gap: why do people act environmentally and what are the barriers to pro-environmental behavior?' *Environmental Education Research,* 8(3), 239–260.

Kumar, A., and Lee, C. M. (2006). 'Retail investor sentiment and return comovements.' *Journal of Finance,* 61(5), 2451–86.

Lavy, V., Ebenstein, A., and Roth, S. (2014). 'The impact of short term exposure to ambient air pollution on cognitive performance and human capital formation (No. w20648)'. *National Bureau of Economic Research Working Paper.* https://doi.org/10.3386/w20648 (accessed October 20, 2023).

Lelieveld, J., Evans, J. S., Fnais, M., Giannadaki, D., and Pozzer, A. (2015). 'The contribution of outdoor air pollution sources to premature mortality on a global scale.' *Nature (London)*, 525(7569), 367–71. https://doi.org/10.1038/nature15371 (accessed October 20, 2023).

Li, J. J., Massa, M., Zhang, H., and Zhang, J. (2021). 'Air pollution, behavioral bias, and the disposition effect in China.' *Journal of Financial Economics*, 142(2), 641–73.

Li, X., Zhang, Q., Zhang, Y., Zhang, L., Wang, Y., Zhang, Q., . . . and He, K. (2017). 'Attribution of PM2.5 exposure in Beijing–Tianjin–Hebei region to emissions: implication to control strategies.' *Science Bulletin,* 62(13), 957–64.

Ma, Yihan. 'China: Online Shoppers 2021.' *Statista*, 14 March 2022, https://www.statista.com/statistics/277391/number-of-online-buyers-in-china/ (accessed October 20, 2023).

Matisoff, D.C., Noonan, D.S., and Flowers, M.E. (2016). 'Policy monitor—Green buildings: Economics and policies.' *Review of Environmental Economics and Policy*, 10(2), 329–46.

Ministry of Ecology and Environment. (2019). 'Environmental inspection results'. https://english.mee.gov.cn/Resources/Reports/soe/SOEE2019/202012/P02020121558745385 98053.pdf (accessed October 20, 2023).

Ministry of Ecology and Environment. (2020). 'Environmental status bulletin of China.' http://english.mee.gov.cn/Resources/Reports/soe/ (accessed October 20, 2023).

Mu, Y., Rubin, E.A., and Zou, E. (2021). 'What's missing in environmental (self-) monitoring: Evidence from strategic shutdowns of pollution monitors (No. w28735)'. *National*

Bureau of Economic Research Working Paper. https://doi.
org/10.3386/w28735 (accessed October 20, 2023).

National Bureau of Statistics. (2020). *China statistical yearbook 2020.*
China Statistics Press.

National Bureau of Statistics. (2021). *China statistical yearbook 2021.*
China Statistics Press.

Neidell, M. (2009). 'Information, avoidance behavior, and health
the effect of ozone on asthma hospitalizations.' *Journal of
Human Resources,* 44(2), 450–78.

Newsham, G.R., Mancini, S., and Birt, B.J. (2009). 'Do LEED-
certified buildings save energy? Yes, but . . .' *Energy and
Buildings,* 41(8), 897–905.

Owens, S. (2000). '"Engaging the public": Information and
Deliberation in Environmental Policy.' *Environment and
Planning A,* 32(7), 1141–1148.

Pan, Y., Qin, Y., Zhang, F., and Zhu, H. (2022). 'Acquiring land in
cold winter: Consequences and possible explanations.' *Journal
of Environmental Economics and Management,* 116.

Panle Jia Barwick, Li, S., Rao, D., and Nahim Bin Zahur. (2018).
'The Morbidity Cost of Air Pollution: Evidence from
Consumer Spending in China.' *IDEAS Working Paper Series
from RePEc.*

Peters, A., Veronesi, B., Calderón-Garcidueñas, L., Gehr, P., Chen,
L.C., Geiser, M., . . . and Schulz, H. (2006). 'Translocation and
potential neurological effects of fine and ultrafine particles a
critical update.' *Particle and Fibre Toxicology,* 3(1), 1–13.

Pope III, C.A. (2000). 'Epidemiology of fine particulate air
pollution and human health: biologic mechanisms and who's
at risk?' *Environmental Health Perspectives,* 108 (suppl 4), 713–23.

Pope III, C.A., Burnett, R.T., Thun, M.J., Calle, E.E.,
Krewski, D., Ito, K., and Thurston, G.D. (2002). 'Lung Cancer,
Cardiopulmonary Mortality, and Long-term Exposure to
Fine Particulate Air Pollution.' *JAMA: the Journal of the*

American Medical Association, 287(9), 1132–1141. https://doi. org/10.1001/jama.287.9.1132 (accessed October 20, 2023).

Pope III, C.A., Burnett, R.T., Thurston, G.D., Thun, M.J., Calle, E.E., Krewski, D., and Godleski, J.J. (2004). 'Cardiovascular mortality and long-term exposure to particulate air pollution: epidemiological evidence of general pathophysiological pathways of disease.' *Circulation,* 109(1), 71–77.

Power, M.C., Weisskopf, M.G., Alexeeff, S.E., Coull, B.A., Spiro, A., and Schwartz, J. (2011). 'Traffic-Related Air Pollution and Cognitive Function in a Cohort of Older Men.' *Environmental Health Perspectives,* 119(5), 682–87.

Power, M.C., Weisskopf, M.G., Alexeeff, S.E., Coull, B.A., Spiro III, A., and Schwartz, J. (2011). 'Traffic-related air pollution and cognitive function in a cohort of older men.' *Environmental Health Perspectives,* 119(5), 682–87.

Power, M.C., Adar, S.D., Yanosky, J.D., Weuve, J., and Spiro III, A. (2018). 'Exposure to air pollution as a potential contributor to cognitive function, cognitive decline, brain imaging, and dementia: A systematic review of epidemiologic research.' *Neurotoxicology* 68, 245–61. DOI: 10.1016/j.neuro.2018.06.007 (accessed October 20, 2023).

Qadri, S. T. (Ed.). (2001). *Fire, smoke, and haze: The ASEAN response strategy.* Asian Development Bank.

Qin, Y., Wu, J., and Yan, J. (2019). 'Negotiating housing deal on a polluted day: Consequences and possible explanations.' *Journal of Environmental Economics and Management,* 94, 161–87.

Ramos, A., Gago, A., Labandeira, X., and Linares, P. (2015). 'The role of information for energy efficiency in the residential sector.' *Energy Economics,* 52, S17–S29.

Sheldon, T. L., and Sankaran, C. (2017). 'The impact of Indonesian forest fires on Singaporean pollution and health.' *American Economic Review,* 107(5), 526–29.

Shenzhen Government Online. (n.d.). 'About Shenzhen.' http://www.sz.gov.cn/en_szgov/aboutsz/ (accessed October 20, 2023).

Simonsohn, U. (2010). 'Weather to go to college.' *The Economic Journal (London)*, 120(543), 270–80. https://doi.org/10.1111/j.1468-0297.2009.02296.x (accessed October 20, 2023).

Singh, T.P., and Visaria, S. (2021). 'Up in the Air: Air Pollution and Crime–Evidence from India.' Working Paper.

State Council of the People's Republic of China. (2013). 'Action Plan on Prevention and Control of Air Pollution Introducing Ten Measures to Improve Air Quality.' https://english.mee.gov.cn/News_service/infocus/201309/t20130924_260707.shtml (accessed October 20, 2023).

Statista. 'China: Average Travel Time for Work by City 2015.' 23 September 2019, https://www.statista.com/statistics/942507/china-average-travel-time-for-work-by-city/ (accessed October 20, 2023).

Suglia, S.F., Gryparis, A., Wright, R.O., Schwartz, J., and Wright, R.J. (2008). 'Association of black carbon with cognition among children in a prospective birth cohort study.' *American Journal of Epidemiology*, 167(3), 280–86.

Sunyer, J., Esnaola, M., Alvarez-Pedrerol, M., Forns, J., Rivas, I., López-Vicente, M., Suades-González, E., Foraster, M., Garcia-Esteban, R., Basagaña, X., Viana, M., Cirach, M., Moreno, T., Alastuey, A., Sebastian-Galles, N., Nieuwenhuijsen, M., and Querol, X. (2015). 'Association between Traffic-Related Air Pollution in Schools and Cognitive Development in Primary School Children: A Prospective Cohort Study: e1001792.' *PloS Medicine*, 12(3). https://doi.org/10.1371/journal.pmed.1001792 (accessed October 20, 2023).

Thaler, R.H. (2015). *Misbehaving: The making of behavioral economics*. W. W. Norton & Company.

Tversky, A., and Kahneman, D. (1981). 'The framing of decisions and the psychology of choice.' *Science*, 211(4481), 453–58

Walls, M., Gerarden, T., Palmer, K., and Bak, X.F. (2017). 'Is energy efficiency capitalized into home prices? Evidence from three US cities.' *Journal of Environmental Economics and Management*, 82, 104–24.

Wang, T.J., Jin, L.S., Li, Z.K., and Lam, K.S. (2000). 'A modeling study on acid rain and recommended emission control strategies in China: Air pollution: placing atmospheric environment in a regional context: Asia and Australasia.' *Atmospheric Environment (1994)*, 34(26), 4467–77.

Weuve, J., Puett, R. C., Schwartz, J., Yanosky, J. D., Laden, F., and Grodstein, F. (2012). 'Exposure to particulate air pollution and cognitive decline in older women.' *Archives of Internal Medicine*, 172(3), 219–27.

World Bank. (2016). 'The Cost of Air Pollution: Strengthening the Economic Case for Action.' *Open Knowledge Repository Beta*. https://openknowledge.worldbank.org/handle/10986/25013 (accessed October 20, 2023).

World Health Organization. (2021). 'Ambient air pollution: Health impacts.'

Xu, J., and Harvey, C.R. (2015). 'The disposition effect and momentum: Evidence from the Chinese stock market.' *Pacific-Basin Finance Journal*, 35, 402–19.

Xu, J., Zhang, Y., Li, M., Lv, D., Zhang, X., Zhu, Y., Zhao, T., Zhang, J., Zhou, L., and Sun, J. (2020). 'Long-term exposure to fine particulate matter affects brain integrity in healthy adults.' *Environmental International* 144, 106012. DOI: 10.1016/j.envint.2020.106012 (accessed October 20, 2023).

Yang, Y (2017). 'Are Green Buildings Really Green? The Energy Efficiency of Green Buildings in Singapore.' *Working Paper*.

Zhang, X., Chen, X., Zhang, X., Guo, J., Zhou, Y., Wu, F., Zhang, Y., and Jin, Y. (2019). 'Short-term effects of ambient PM2.5 and PM10 on cognitive performance in healthy young adults.' *Environmental Science and Pollution Research*, 26, 34119-34128. DOI: 10.1007/s11356-019-06687-w (accessed October 20, 2023)

Zhang, X., Jin, Y., Dai, H., Xie, Y., and Zhang, S. (2019). 'Health and economic benefits of cleaner residential heating in the Beijing–Tianjin–Hebei region in China.' *Energy Policy*, 127, 165–78.

Zou, E.Y. (2021). 'Unwatched pollution: The effect of intermittent monitoring on air quality.' *American Economic Review*, 111(7), 2101–26. https://doi.org/10.1257/aer.20181346